THIS TRIBE OF MINE

A Story of Anglo-Saxon
Viking Culture in America

George Hiram Williston

Published by:
Williston and Robbins Publishing
P.O. Box 137
Shelbyville, MI 49344

ISBN: 978-0-9815445-0-2

FSC

Mixed Sources
Product group from well-managed
forests, controlled sources and
recycled wood or fiber

Cert no. SW-COC-002283
www.fsc.org
© 1996 Forest Stewardship Council

Book Editor: Bruce Madden, braineros@att.net
Cover Design: Janet Shelby, rovergraphics.com

Front Cover: A reproduction of a helmet from an Anglo-Saxon burial site at Sutton Hoo, England late 600s A.D.

Printed in the United States of America.

Table of Contents

This book is dedicated to the spirit and memory
of Dr. Martin Luther King, Jr.
who spoke so powerfully and intelligently
for peace and justice for all mankind.

Introduction

Today, many tribal people struggle to maintain their ancient languages. Each group's unique native tongue and set of symbols help preserve their cultural heritage and unique vision of the world.

This connection between language and culture is of major importance to this story. I define culture as the accepted normal attitudes and behaviors of a particular geographical group of people, speaking a particular language.

As the son of a social psychologist, I grew up in the USA during the Vietnam War years. Those turbulent times left me with a major question: Why is our American culture so militaristic and competitive while a large number of people in our culture claim to follow the teachings of Jesus Christ?

Many years ago I began a personal quest for answers to resolve this paradox, a quest that resonated with the feelings in my heart. I followed the trail back 1500 years to the roots of the language I speak today. The path led to mainland Germany, the home of the Angles and Saxons. This is the historic place of origin for the English language, the dominant American culture, and its policies.

Growing up an ordinary American Midwestern boy, I

found many surprises in the history *not* taught to me in public school. For example, the English language did not originate on the island of Britain. It rowed over to that island from mainland Germany with my ancestors in their Viking boats. My surname Williston is of Saxon origin. These are my people.

As I learned more about my ancient *Aenglish* bloodline and the tribe that gave us the English language we speak today, I began to understand my behavior and the actions of my English-American ancestors. The policies of our government (past and present) are in my opinion just an extension of these *Aenglish* cultural values. We, in the United States of America are the inheritors of a Viking culture regardless of earlier ancestral origins. And, that culture has been and *is* warlike and very competitive.

Like most words in our language ending with -ing, Viking is truly a verb although my dictionary claims it to be a person from the north. Viking as a verb is the action of a group of armed men going out, usually by boat, to secure by whatever means necessary the resources they desire. In the old days it was land, gold, women, slaves, and glory.

Anglo-Saxons developed so-called divinely justified social rankings. A few families were said to be direct descendants of God (*Woden*) followed by an honored professional warrior class who protected them. There was constant and fierce competition between the different but related tribes. The losers who survived (usually women and children) became slaves to the victors, to be sold or used as personal slaves. This inter-tribal warfare led to a huge slave class that existed until around 1100 A.D. This period of slavery is virtually unmentioned by Anglo-Saxon and English historians.

The primary social tenets (folkways) that are the foundation for our cultural beliefs of right and wrong behavior came from these Anglo-Saxon people. And, our social structure somewhat moderated over time has its origins within these tribes' rigid hierarchies of wealth, entitlement, divinity notions and power.

The competitive relationships we live, the notion of getting ahead of our fellow citizen by controlling as much wealth, land, or labor as possible, leads to a class of aristocrats and working poor. We still see the world through Viking eyes, viewing those cultures that do not hoard wealth in the same fashion or make fine iron weapons as child-like and ripe for exploitation.

The basic structure of our society has evolved from this Viking principle: A few on top enjoy the benefits granted by God while those below do the work in this divinely-ordained scheme.

We have within our society the admired male warrior hero who can dominate the world with his superior weapons and the corporate CEO who dominates wealth.

This is the Viking culture. It is has been moving through time, blending into our country's cultural and social tenets and values since the Pilgrims landed.

We are (active or passive) participants in this culture. We know people enter and leave the social hierarchy under varying circumstances, but the cultural structure rarely changes. What our culture defines as right and how we personally act on that belief is truly important. We are a part of an ancient tradition of domination and our country's representatives are acting out old Viking values upon the world each day, with little change from past behavior.

With superior military weapons and an attitude of superiority grounded in Manifest Destiny, we conquered the estimated 60 million original people of this continent, we brought in African slaves, and gradually we launched larger iron ships, sending them forth to enforce our business interests.

In The United States of America, the cultural notion of winners and losers defines our viewpoint of working people, minorities, and children. Teachers are taught that the numerical ranking of the Bell curve represents a normal distribution of students within the classroom with a few on top and many below. Our public education system re-enforces the notion of winners and losers through its competitive ranking model.

In our own country, 10% of the population controls 75% of the wealth. Our dominant culture teaches us this is normal. There are after all winners and losers, rich and poor: each group receives what they deserve according to this viewpoint.

I see this dominant cultural paradigm as the leading cause of social unrest in the world today. Dominated people naturally resist. People dominated by violence and the dominators themselves both become brutalized by this philosophy.

Our attempts to exploit and dominate the natural world are leading to the permanent loss of plant and animal species. While we deplete resources with little or no restraint, this adversarial relationship with nature is damaging the worldwide ecosystem. The effects of manmade pollution harm the Earth's environment.

Is this a healthy way to live? Should our past be our future? Should we be living in the world today like my Anglo-Saxon ancestors? Should the warriors who have the weapons and the drive control the resources? Should we believe that the creator of all life on this earth raised some individuals or racial groups to a favored status, granting them privileges that are denied other individuals or groups?

There are teachings from the past that we should heed in the present. Can a fresh look at these teachings inspire peace among all peoples of the world? Will the words spoken by Jesus the Christ, *Buddha*, Hindu *mahatmas*, and the teachings of many native peoples whose cultures promote peace and co-operation take us on that journey? There are ways to change the future by following a different way of being human that is more cooperative and loving.

It is not my intention to judge the people of the past. They were the heroes of their own people, acting within the flow of their own cultural paradigm, struggling for what they believed to be right. Most of us believe we are doing honorable things based upon context within our society or culture.

History however has been written by the scribes of victorious male warriors, capturing in words and pictures the various battles waged for freedom and domination throughout recorded history. These tales relating the heroics of battle and the accompanying hero worship have been validated in textbooks used by our public school systems. The books typically represent history from the victor's perspective, a perspective that may reflect fragmentary one-sided stories rather than a more complete record of an imperfect past.

My goals in the book are twofold. The early chapters begin with a compassionate look at *arstory* (our story), a brief, more inclusive re-examination of the Anglo-Saxon *Aenglish* heritage we all share either through direct lineage or by its imposition upon the willing and unwilling members of our society. Generally, throughout this study, I respectfully acknowledge both sides of the story regarding those people trampled in the tribal expansion out of Germany. I am confident that by showing where our culture is rooted, compassionately and openly facing this history of domination, examining the costs of that domination, and looking at healthier ways of being, we can change this Viking mindset and have a better, more peaceful tomorrow.

The second goal is to transmit hope to all readers of this book that we are part of something larger than all this cultural chaos that surrounds us. We are part of a universe saturated with intelligence. There have been and will continue to be many great teachers who have tried and will try to redirect us toward the path of higher human potential. These teachers have tried to show us who we could *be* as human *beings* interacting with this great intelligent force surrounding us. These simple peaceful voices may not always be heard above the loud, aggressive, ever-present ego-driven barkers but their voices remain a constant. Listen for them.

If we examine and understand a past culture that seems to be guiding our present worldview, I hope we can open a dialog for change here on Earth. I do not accept the philosophy: "It's always been this way," meaning there can be no change. I believe it is our task to open our hearts and put our minds together to build a better future, living lives in balance with the web of life around us. I hope to provide you additional clues to follow on *your* quest to find truth and understanding. It is an exciting time.

George Hiram Williston
Michigan August 2007

1

The Landing
Of The Seawolves

The more than 6 billion people inhabiting Earth are each part of a social, cultural continuum stretching from the ancient past to our present day. I am an American Anglo-Saxon. My ancient Anglo-Saxon ancestors were part of a violent warrior slaving culture, who beseeched their warrior-deities *Woden* and *Thor* for the necessary strength in combat to slaughter their enemies. Competition among Anglo-Saxon warrior tribes was a way of life.

The passage of time lulls us into a belief that cultures are vastly different in the present than those which existed in the remote past. In truth, changes in day-to-day life largely encompass little more than habits of convenience. Societies both ancient and modern were (and are) highly resistant to change. As the old saying goes, "Those who ignore the past are doomed to repeat it."

I seek to explore issues within our society by bringing to

light the ancient roots of these cultural behaviors. Many questions arise: What is the origin of the perception that we as Americans have the right to and must be THE dominant global culture? From whom have we inherited these ideas? Why is American culture so uniquely involved with and touched by violence? What legacy do we pass on to our children? Why in a country that is so rich are there so many who have so little? Why does the struggle for civil rights continue to meet such resistance? Why is 75 percent of the wealth in our country controlled by only 10 percent of the people? Why are these resources concentrated in the hands of so few? Is this the best way to live and be human?

In warrior societies the victor wins the ability to tell *his story* as history. A broader world-perspective hints that there are at least two sides to every drama, and sometimes many more. History as we commonly know it is the tale of those who emerge victorious; those who are killed or conquered have not typically been allowed to tell their side of the story. This leads us to a narrow view of who we are (or were) and what we (or our forebears) have done (or had done to them) in the world.

Language is the transmitter of culture. It is nothing more than a group of symbolic sounds with commonly agreed-upon meanings. However these sounds have power. The ideas these collective sounds represent, define how the speakers view the world around them and offer us clues how people see themselves within that world.

Our language is named for and attributed to England, but did not originate there. It came, in fact, to Briton with warriors from Germany. At first this fact seems odd, as we associate the dominant American origins directly with Great Britain. Mention ancient British peoples and, to most Americans, the automatic mental image is of the Celts. This is somewhat accurate

2

though the Celts did not speak English or any offshoot of it. They spoke a Gaelic language. This ancient tongue survived a long Roman occupation that destroyed much of their Druid spirituality but the Gaelic language was not displaced until the invasion of the Anglo-Saxons. After much bloody warfare, beginning around the time of Christ the native Britons fell under control of the Roman legions. The Romans ruled over much of what came to be England for more than four centuries.

In the first century after Christ's death, the Romans scouted deep into Germany. The historian *Tacitus* observed the folk there to be generally large-framed, red-haired and blue-eyed. Their country, he noted, was not abundant in anything but was a northland where scarcity was common. The way of life for these Germans was defined by this scarcity, forcing them to carefully utilize their resources, making do with what little they had within the boundaries of their own tribes.

The men *Tacitus* encountered were warrior-farmers and heavy drinkers who treated their wives and daughters with respect (at least from a Roman's perspective). He noted those men listened to their wives' advice. He refers to average males as freedmen. These freedmen possessed slaves who lived as tenant farmers. These tribes had hereditary royalty, though a tribal group's true leaders would have proven themselves in battle. Women and children followed their men to the battle, yelling encouragement (origin of cheerleading), reminding husbands and fathers that they did not wish to end their lives as slaves. In wedding ceremonies, a woman was instructed that, "She is her husband's partner in toil and danger, and to dare with him alike in war." Adultery was rare, and women married only once, brought up to love not so much the man as the married state. "To limit the number of one's offspring was accounted an infamy," recorded *Tacitus*. "In every household the children, naked and filthy, grow up with those stout frames and limbs which we so admire."

By 410 A.D. Rome could no longer adequately support her legions in the West and called them home to defend the Roman capital against a Goth invasion. With their government and military gone, Briton's original inhabitants were without organized protection from raiders. Villages to the south, between Scotland and *Lundinium* (London's vicinity) were highly vulnerable and *Pict* (Scottish) tribes raided south past Hadrian's Wall. Wealthy Britons on the coast hired mercenaries who roamed the Channel to turn back these attackers. These hired warriors were of the Anglo-Saxon tribes, tough people who would become the rootstock of our English/*Aenglish* (and hence influence much of our American) culture.

John Richard Green was born and schooled in Oxford. He published his seminal *Short History of the English People* in 1916, and his work begins this way:

> For the fatherland of the English race we must look far away from England itself. In the fifth century after the birth of Christ, the one country which we know to have borne the name Angeln or Engleland lay in the district which we now call Sleswick, a district in the heart of the peninsula which parts the Baltic from the northern seas . . . the dwellers in this district, however, seem to have been merely an outlying fragment of what was called the Engle or English folk, the bulk of whom lay probably along the middle Elbe and on the Weser. To the north of the English in their Sleswick home lay another kindred tribe, the Jutes, whose name is still preserved in their district of Jutland. To the south of them a number of German tribes had drawn together in their homeland between the Elbe and the Ems, and a wide tract across the Ems to the Rhine, into the people of the Saxons.

Engle, Saxon, and Jute all belonged to the same Low branch of the Teutonic family: and at the moment history discovers them, they were being drawn together by the ties of common blood, common speech, common social and political institutions. Each of them was destined to share in the conquest of the land in which we live: and it is from the union of all of them, when its conquest was complete, that the English people have sprung.

We do not know whether it was the pressure of other tribes or the example of their German brethren, who were now moving in general attack on the Empire from their forest homes, or simply the barrenness of their coast which drove the hunters, farmers and fishermen of the English tribes to the sea. But the daring spirit of their race already broke out in the secrecy and suddenness of their swoop, in the fierceness of their onset, in the careless glee with which they seized either sword or oar. "Foes they are," sang a Roman poet of the time, "fierce beyond other foes, and cunning as they are fierce; the sea is their school of war, and the storm is their friend; they are seawolves that live on the pillage of the world."

Green's assertion then, is that the English culture's most influential ancestors were Germanic Vikings. Viking is a word associated with dwellers in Northern Europe. The Northman Viking culture did not stop at the modern boundaries of Norway or Sweden. It was also present in Denmark, Germany, and the Netherlands in early times.

These Vikings or as a Roman poet romantically characterized them, seawolves rowed thirty-foot open boats from the coastal regions of Germany down through the English Channel. Each band headed by a dominant warrior male who led his group into battle was also comprised of family members and friends. Initially hired by the Britons these Anglo-Saxon seawolves were offered supplies (and who knows what else) to fight the *Picts*. They may have been exiles, as it was customary for the Viking tribes to occasionally expel some of their own. These newcomers were also farmers and liked the fertile soil they found. Within a very short period of time, they plotted to make their own place on the island.

During the mercenary period of these Viking raids, the warriors took slaves and generally plundered those around them whenever possible. Thus, any outsiders with whom they came into contact were at considerable risk including those Britons who hired them for military assistance.

Over the next 200 years these warriors and their descendents commenced what we would call genocide against the island's original inhabitants. The invaders referred to the islands' indigenous people as *welas* (welsh), their own term for foreigner or slave. These unfortunate natives were eventually pushed south and west seeking refuge in mountainous regions they could more readily defend. This geographic spur would come to be known as Wales, its fiercely independent people speaking an offshoot of the original Gaelic—even as they do in the present day.

The Anglo-Saxon people involved in this conquest had only a very basic written language known as runes. Those first records of events that still exist were written many years afterward by a few monks on the island. The accuracy of these stories is suspect, being based on legend retold at the time. The Anglo-Saxon invaders retold events through song and the etching of rune marks on sticks. The Christian monks who later made more detailed descriptions written in Latin were *Bede*, *Gildas*, and *Nennius*. Historians such as the aforementioned Green and Sir Frank Stenton have closely examined the first two monks. The voice of *Nennius* is the only early writer to represent the Welsh perspective, those original people of the island who were killed and eventually displaced by the Anglo-Saxons. *Nennius* contributed a different viewpoint on this conquest of ancient Briton.

Anglo Saxon Chronicles

The conquerors' side of the story was written in an early form of the English language in the late 800's, appearing as the *Anglo-Saxon Chronicles*. The Saxon monarch, *King Aelfred* commissioned the writing of these documents. He was the first Anglo-Saxon ruler to consolidate the kingship over all Anglo-Saxons on the island. *Aelfred* had a curiosity about ancient writings and spent a great deal of time studying them. This man plainly understood the importance of bringing history forward into the present for the future. The *Anglo-Saxon Chronicles* represent the earliest written snapshot of the *Aenglish* self-image. I use this term *Aenglish* as a transitional word for the culture more closely associated with *Angleland* that became England.

Nine of the original *Chronicle* documents are still in existence, each varying slightly from the others. The antiquated language of these stories must be translated into more modern English form. Pieces of old words may not be immediately apparent today but they are relics of this forgotten heritage; the –*ton* suffix, for instance (as in Williston, Stenton, or Washington) refers to the moat or defensive ring around a Saxon village.

The *Chronicles* begin with *Gaius Julius'* invasion of the Briton's island in 60 B.C., making immediate reference to the birth of Jesus. Christian and Viking culture are blended together throughout its pages. The insertions of important Christian religious dates between episodes of war and massacre are noteworthy.

Aethelbert or Ethelbert was the first Anglo-Saxon royal to claim Christian baptism in 598 A.D., after a reign of over 30 years. Another striking feature of the *Chronicles* is even 300 winters later, those responsible for writing the *Chronicles* still referred to their early tribal kings as descendants of *Woden*. What does such a blending say? A Viking cultural memory remained intact even as the tenets of the Christian church became entwined with the earlier Anglo-Saxon culture. What ensued was a blending of Viking and Christian ideologies. The Angles and Saxons merged seamlessly into warrior Christians.

The following excerpts from the *Anglo-Saxon Chronicles* clearly reveal the heroes of the warrior Christian archetype in the sequentially organized entries:

A.D. 443
This year sent the Britons over the sea to Rome, and begged assistance against the Picts; but they had none, for the Romans were at war with Attila, king of the Huns. Then sent they to the Angles, and requested the same from the nobles of that nation.

A.D. 449
This year Marcian and Valentinian assumed the empire, and reigned seven winters. In their days Hengest and Horsa, invited by Wurtgern, king of the Britons to his assistance, landed in Britain in a place that is called Ipwinesfleet; first of all to support the Britons, but they afterwards fought against them. The king directed them to fight against the Picts; and they did so; and obtained the victory wheresoever they came. They then sent to the Angles, and desired them to send more assistance. They described the worthlessness of the Britons, and the richness of the land. They then sent them greater support. Then came the men from the three powers of Germany; the Old Saxons, the Angles, and the Jutes. From the Jutes

are descended the men of Kent, the Wightwarians (that is, the tribe that now dwelleth in the Isle of Wight), and that kindred in Wessex that men yet call the kindred of the Jutes. From Anglia, which has ever since remained waste between the Jutes and the Saxons, came the East Angles, the Middle Angles, the Mercians, and all of those north of the Humber. Their leaders were two brothers, Hengest and Horsa; who were the sons of Wihtgils; Wihtgils was the son of Witta, Witta of Wecta, Wecta of Woden. From this Woden arose all our royal kindred, and that of Southumbrians also.

A.D. 455
This year Hengest and Horsa fought with Wurtgern the king on the spot that is called Aylesford. His brother Horsa being there slain, Hengest afterwards took to the kingdom with his son Esc.

A.D. 457
This year Hengest and Esc fought with the Britons on the spot that is called Crayford, and there slew four thousand men. The Britons then forsook the land of Kent, and in great consternation fled to London.

A.D. 465
This year Hengest and Esc fought with the Welsh, nigh Wippedfleet, and there slew twelve leaders, all Welsh. On their side a thane was there slain, whose name was Wipped.

A.D. 473
This year Hengest and Esc fought with the Welsh, and took immense booty. And the Welsh fled the English like fire.

A.D. 477
This year came Ella to Britain, with his three sons, Cymen, and Wienking, and Cissa, in three ships; landing at a place that is called Cymenshore. There they slew

many of the Welsh; and some in flight they drove into the wood that is called Andred'sley.

A.D. 482

This year the blessed Abbot Benedict shone in this world, by the splendor of those virtues which the blessed Gregory records in the Book of Dialogues.

A.D. 490

This year Ella and Cissa besieged the city of Andred, and slew all that were therein; nor was one Briton left there afterwards.

A.D. 508

This year Cerdic and Cynric slew a British king, whose name was Natanleod, and five thousand men with him. After this was the land named Netley, from him, as far as Charford.

A.D. 509

This year, St. Benedict, the abbot, father of all the monks ascended to heaven.

A.D. 514

This year came the West-Saxons into Britain, with three ships, at the place that is called Cerdic's-ore. And Stuff and Wihtgar fought with the Britons and put them to flight.

A.D. 519

This year Cerdic and Cynric undertook the government of the West- Saxons; the same year they fought with the Britons at a place now called Charford. From that day have reigned the children of the West- Saxon kings.

A.D. 530

This year Cerdic and Cynric took the Isle of Wight, and slew many men in Carisbrook.

A.D. 552

This year Cynric fought with the Britons on the spot that is called Sarum, and put them to flight. Cerdic was the father of Cynric. Cerdic was the son of Elesa, Elesa of Esla, Esla of Gewis, Gewis of Wye, Wye of Frewin, Frewin of Frithgar, Frithgar of Brand, Brand of Balday, Balday of Woden. In this year Ethelbert, the son of Erminric, was born, who on the two and thirtieth year of his reign received the rite of baptism, the first of all the kings in Britain.

Nennius The Father Of The Arthurian Legend

Nennius, representing the Celt Briton viewpoint, composed his 8th Century *Historia Brittonum* in Latin, the only developed written language known on the island at the time. In his account, the native people were not easily defeated, but rather won many battles against the invaders that he named Saxons. The monk also wrote of the King Arthur legend. He described in the *Historia Brittonum* a valiant leader who fought with all his heart to maintain his culture's independence. The Arthur he depicted, an elected military leader, fought twelve battles, killing 960 Saxons in one charge at Mount Baden.

The monk *Nennius* also provided an account of the origin of the people that lived on the British Isle at the time of the conquest. He may have written this version from an oral legend that was commonly accepted truth. "At the time of the Saxon invasion," he wrote, "the inhabitants of the island may have come from Greek or Roman roots long before *Caesar*, and the name Brit comes from the family of *Brutus*." The Scottish *Picts*, according to this historian, ". . . occupied the Orkney Islands, whence they laid waste to many regions and seized those on the left-hand side of Britain, where they still remain, keeping possession of a third part . . . the Scots arrived in Ireland from Spain."

During this early period of raiding by *Picts* and Scots, the first of the longboats began to arrive from Northwestern Germany. An explanation for the invaders' eventual dominance is recorded by *Nennius* (with my emphasis italicized): "And let him that reads understand that the Saxons were victorious, and ruled Britain, not from superior prowess, but *on account of the great sins of the Britons; God so permitted it.*"

Nennius is careful to outline exactly where and how these fatal British sins led to their eventual conquest. During *Vortigern's* rule (called *"Wurtgern"* in the *Anglo-Saxon Chronicles*. *Hengest* and *Horsa* were offered clothing and supplies to turn back the *Picts* from their raiding. When this was accomplished *Vortigern* had no further need of them, and let it be known to the Saxons that it was time to leave. At this point a practice that would become a repeated cultural characteristic in struggles with native peoples comes to light: The use of alcohol, temptation, and trickery in treaty negotiation. Having been told his services were no longer required and that he should leave, *Hengist* came up with a new idea to trap his onetime host into a formal agreement. *Hengist* had a beautiful daughter. He was aware of *Vortigern's* lusty habits, and so commanded that a feast be laid with ample wine and ale. During this party *Vortigern* became intoxicated and demanded the young woman; *Hengist* allowed it, but only in exchange for the province of *Cient* (Kent). A drunken deal was struck. Now that he was part of the family, *Hengist* soon sent for forty more ships filled with friends.

In the sordid aftermath, as the story goes, *Vortigern* had several wives, marrying even his own daughter by another woman, producing a son who was raised by *Saint Germanus* as an early man of the church. *Vortigern* also sired numerous other offspring by different mothers, some of whom, like *Vortimer*, rose up to fight the droves of now-invited but unwanted relatives.

Hengist, not content with the county he had been given by *Vortigern* formulated another plan for full consolidation of his power. He offered aging *Vortigern* perpetual friendship and peace, calling for a new treaty and another feast to celebrate it. Both sides attended with equal numbers of men. They ate and drank heavily and talked of peace. Then, at a prescribed moment, *Hengist* yelled *"Nimed eure Saxes!"* (Long live Saxons!). Each Saxon drew a knife and drove it into the Briton seated next to him. The only person spared was a much-sobered *Vortigern*, who was ransomed back to his family.

Having fully described the transgressions that led to the Britons' demise, *Nennius* relates that *Hengist* and *Horsa* believed themselves descended from *"Godwulf* the great, who, as they say, was the son of a god, not the omnipotent God and our Lord Jesus Christ, but the offspring of one of their idols whom, blinded by some demon (*Wodin* had one eye), they worshipped according to the custom of the heathen."

Little is known of the Anglo-Saxon ancient religious cosmology because it was absorbed into Christianity before its practitioners had a developed written language. According to John Green, the English historian, quoted earlier:

"The religion of the English was the same as that of the whole German family. Christianity, which had by this time brought about the conversion of the Roman Empire, had not penetrated as yet among the forests of the North. Our own names for the days of the week still recall to us the gods whom our forefathers worshipped. Wednesday is the day of *Woden*, the war-god, the guardian of ways and boundaries, the inventor of letters (runes), the common god of the whole conquering people, whom every tribe held to be the first ancestor of its kings. Thursday is the day of Thunder, or as the Northmen called him, Thor, the god of air and storm and rain; as Friday is Frea's-day, the god of peace and joy and fruitfulness . . ."

However, the religion of the Vikings did survive in other Norse cultures especially Greenland where more information is available about their earlier beliefs.

Woden (Odin, *Voutan*) was the dominant god believed to have created first the Earth with the help of his two brothers and then man and woman from the ash and elm trees. He was a poet who could recite long epics and a shaman who shape-shifted to interact with humans in the earthly realms. He was thought to have one eye missing allowing him to see the visible realms with the existing eye and the invisible realms with the blinded eye. He was quick to anger and grantor of the so-called beserker rage to warriors in battle. Such divine rage allowed a man to kill like a wild man untouched by enemy weapons. He had a cult following known as the wearers of the bear shirt who sought this ability. He was the collector of souls.

Thunar (Thor) was one of his children from union with one of the giant race believed to represent earth. *Thunar* caused the thunder and lightening with his war hammer whenever he rolled across the sky to protect the Earth from the race of giants. His thunder and lightening bring fertility to the soil. He was thought of as protector and the symbol of male fertility bestowed upon earth, the receptacle. *Woden's* wife was called *Frigg* or *Frija*. Another son of *Woden* was known as *Twia* who had lost one hand in mythological battle. *Twia* was the God of War. The names of our days of the week are taken from these ancient gods' names: *Twiasday* (Tuesday); *Wodens-day* (Wednesday); *Thorsday* (Thursday); *Friasday* (Friday).

The ancient Germanic tribes had sacred groves of trees where they gathered for ritual, much like the (pre-Roman) Gaelic-speaking peoples on the British island. *Tacitus* recorded many tribes by name, but of the Saxons, Angles, and Jutes, only the Angles are mentioned. He wrote about their beliefs and characteristics:

> "What on the contrary ennobles the Langobards is the smallness of their number, for they, who are surrounded with very many and very powerful nations, derive their security from no obsequiousness or plying; but from the dint of battle and adventurous deeds. There follow in order the Reudignians, and Aviones, and Angles, and Varinians, and Eudoses, and Suardones and Nuithones; all defended by rivers and forests. Nor in one of these nations does aught remarkable occur, only that they universally join the worship of Herthum; that is to say, the Mother Earth. Her they believe to interpose in the affairs of man, and to visit countries. In an island of the ocean stands the wood Castum: in it is a chariot dedicated to the Goddess, covered over with a curtain, permitted to be touched by none but a Priest."

Somewhere between these divergent perspectives of Anglo-Saxon social and religious history is the truth about my ancestors. It is interesting to me that the hard details of what happened in this conquest are virtually unknown. As conquerors, their side of the story is the only one considered within our culture, and this is usually described as a migration. The *Aenglish* are presented as wanderers who found and settled a beautiful land. The original language of the island was nearly extinguished much like the languages of Native Americans in North America. Genetic research done in part by Mark Thomas of The Centre for Genetic Anthropology, University of London showed a significant difference between central English males and Welsh males when compared to Frisian male DNA (more closely akin to the Anglo-Saxons continental ancestors). The huge body of people who inhabited the island when the Anglo-Saxons arrived were discounted as foreigners, killed, enslaved, or driven away to the far edges of the region.

Here, then, is the basis of our dominant cultural heritage. From these people emerged the English language and the cultural constructs of the English and American people, which today we see in the militaristic corporate quest for wealth. The Anglo-Saxon warriors sought riches, slaves, land and glory in battle—above all else. How much of their warrior ethos remains with us? Each group of Saxons believed that *they* had God on their side, that *they* (rather than the Britons) were privileged as his true descendents. *Nennius*, in turn, believed that the original British people were punished by his almighty, having offended him with their wicked ways.

My ancestors who invaded and conquered foreign peoples did so because of daring, aggression and the technical ability to produce swift boats and good iron weapons. The importance of the craftsmanship of iron and wood should not be understated here. Iron changed everything. The ability to form iron and a willingness to use it in war became a social tenant of the Vikings. They were proud of their dominance obtained through skillful usage of superior weaponry. These practices somehow developed as adaptive in a harsh northern environment among groups of similar aggressive people. As worshipers of *Woden,* my people lived by the sword and the pike. They respected only those who lived the same way.

The authors of the *Anglo-Saxon Chronicles* recorded in

writing the tribal legend including how Anglo-Saxon warriors destroyed whole encampments or entire towns, slaughtering the inhabitants without a trace of remorse. These raiding tribes divided the land they took in relation to their status as warriors within their tribe. Their warrior leaders were portioned a greater share of the plunder and assumed ownership of the conquered regions. Four centuries after their arrival, the forebears of our own dominant culture centralized themselves under *Aelfred's* rule and began to record their version of what transpired. To this day we still see the world through the cultural framework of these ancestral eyes. I tell this story not to glamorize what occurred long ago but to confront who we are today so that we may learn from the past.

The following is a Viking poem of the day about *Harald Hardrada*, onetime King of Norway who died by Anglo-Saxon hands. The poem clearly expresses the Viking way, a story of violence and plunder perhaps not so different from the violent conquests recorded in our own more recent history.

Harald, you ravaged Zealand, you gave the helmets
hard work to bear; shields were burst asunder.
Fiercely the fires burned in the farms of Roskilde:
the warrior king made the ruined houses glow.
The countrymen lay fallen: Hel the goddess of death
had robbed them of their freedom.
Those who lived fled,
bent with anguish, to the forests.
The fairest women were seized:
the lock held the maiden's body.
You sent before you many unwilling women to the ships:
the fair-skinned bore the chains.
The grey eagles' keen claws, oh king, you dyed in blood,
the wolf always fed before you went homeward!

Harald's rule ended abruptly when he met a Viking's death in England in 1066 A.D., slain at the Battle of Stamford Bridge.

In 2007, the history of America's place in the world is the tale of an old, old story repeated more than once throughout our history as a nation. The world is ailing under a model of resource hoarding and militarism. It is time to expose the source of these cultural attitudes and recognize them as philosophies that should be left in the past, leaving us with hope for a better, healthier cooperative society in the future. The rush for wealth and resources is dysfunctional for the planet and all its inhabitants. We must embrace cooperation among individuals, cultures and nations. The transition from aggressive competition to cooperation is a slow one and tough to fuel but its time has come.

In the beginning of the 21st Century, America is still sending huge naval and air armadas to distant shores. These floating naval iron cities are loaded with the latest weapons technology and many warriors. There are currently 725 American military bases around the world. Nearly half of our national discretionary budget (equaling the rest of the world's *military* budgets put together) maintains this huge military effort. Dominance through superior firepower is our unspoken slogan and in many cases it is used to protect large corporate interests abroad securing cheap labor and resources. Are we the modern equivalent of those ancient violent raiders, the sea-wolves?

2

Tribal Roots Of The Aenglish Social Structure

Each individual born into the world, beginning with early infancy, learns right from wrong based upon those credible figures he or she discovers as authoritative voices, usually a mother and a father in the home and later when we leave the home, teachers, older children, young adults, among others. From these early role models we construct frameworks of values, proper modes of speech and self-expression, identities that fit within a larger group, and the social precepts of a particular cultural backdrop.

When we're very young we have little choice in the development of our individual cultural identities, being unable to choose credible figures to teach us. As we mature, we gradually gain the freedom to choose role models who make the most sense to us. By the time we reach full mental development, however, most people have absorbed and operate with the social norms practiced by those who brought them up.

Whatever the background from which we emerge, the majority of human beings re-enact a continuation of the cultural lifestyle with which they are most familiar. Rewards or punishments are frequently used to help shape us to fit within the cultural environment. The philosophies, heroes, and language surrounding us during childhood development form our life-patterns. The fear of not belonging, being excluded from the group, has a powerful effect upon a person's actions and emotions. We are social animals with a strong need for acceptance, to feel a part of a group. We do not do well alone. Human contact and company is essential for healthy development and happiness.

To one degree or another, all social groups think of themselves as the standard, the center. Outsiders are viewed as different and less significant. We think our way is the best way and others should act like us. We are a very judgmental people. As a teacher in public schools I see how young people treat one another. I see in so many ways the competitive ranking of individuals and their reactions to such ranking. These are young people waking up to the values of the larger culture. It is psychologically ingrained in us to believe that our way of life is natural and that those with differing customs are misguided. This is an expression of a social construct called ethnocentricity.

Our culture is based primarily on competition. This is how wage earners, athletes, employers, schools, companies, students, and CEO's relate to each other. Within this structure the individual struggles to acquire wealth and, consequently, an upward mobility tied to power. The more material wealth you have, the higher you are rated in the social hierarchy of America. The more wealth a man controls, the more influence he exerts, the more he is revered (or resented) by those who have less. A person's identity is closely related to what this person owns. Such a model—the selfish controlling of available resources beyond basic daily necessities—is a wide plank in our social platform. We grow up seeing this competition depicted as an entirely normal healthy natural way of life.

Cultural behavior patterns, even in this technological age, are not newly invented every week, but in fact are rooted in very old ideas with only surface adaptations to fit the modern world. We bring ancient cultural constructs from the past to interact with present-day events in ways we are not consciously aware. Let's examine the distant past once more for clues to our behavior.

Early Anglo-Saxon Slavery

As the Roman *Tacitus* observed, around the time of Christ, the Germanic tribes were country-dwellers who occupied mud-plastered homes dug into the earth, tilling an expanse of ground in common with other related family groups. They buried food in caches against the threat of winter, covering them with cow dung so that marauders might not easily discover them. They kept slaves.

Tacitus described the kind of slavery he witnessed in early Germany as a tenant-farmer relationship in which the tenant was not permitted to leave.

> ". . . slaves are not employed after our manner with the distinct domestic duties assigned to them, but each has the management of a house and home of his own. The master requires from the slave a certain quantity of grain, of cattle, and of clothing, as he would from a tenant, and this is the limit of subjection. All other household functions are discharged by the wife and children. To strike a

21

slave or to punish him with bonds or with hard labor is a rare occurrence. They often kill them, not in enforcing strict discipline, but on the impulse of passion, as they would an enemy, only it is done with impunity."

Former Reading University Professor of History and author, Sir Frank Stenton published his Oxford Press *Anglo-Saxon England* in 1943, with reprints following in 1975 and 2001. The work is a careful examination of "The Age of Migration," the Anglo-Saxon invasion of Britain, providing a detailed account of noble bloodlines and important dates regarding the ruling class. Stenton's perspective demonstrates how entrenched many historians have been with the Saxon conquerors' viewpoint, while hardly mentioning the early Britons who were killed or displaced. In the book's 730 pages of text (or 812 in the latest edition) five sentences are devoted to the slave trade, including this representative selection:

> "The institution of slavery was part of earliest English law, and in view of later evidence there can be no doubt that the primitive English *ceorl* was usually a slave owner."

These *ceorls* were independent freemen farmers, heads of household in the common class.

The earliest written English laws are the called Dooms. *Aethelberht*, King of Kent recorded 85 laws around 600 AD. These laws of *Aethelberht* outline payment of money as retribution for crimes and directed who was to receive the payment. There are also references to slavery. The Dooms are the earliest reference point of our legal heritage. Here are chosen excerpts from the Medieval Sourcebook found online at fordham.edu:

6. If anyone slay a freeman, fifty shillings to the king, as *drihtinbeah* (payment).
10. If a man lie with the king's maiden, let him pay a *bot* (compensation) of fifty shillings.
11. If she be a grinding slave, let him pay a *bot* of twenty-five shillings. The third (class), twelve shillings.
16. If a man lie with the *ceorl's birele* (steward-servant), let him make *bot* with six shillings, with a slave of the second (class), fifty *scaetts* (20th of a shilling); with one of the third, thirty *scaetts*.
17. If any one be the first to make an inroad into a man's *tun* (home-village), let him make *bot* with six shillings; let him who follows, with three shillings; after, each a shilling.
31. If a freeman lie with a freeman's wife, let him pay for it with his *wergild* (money value of his life), and provide another wife with his own money, and bring her to the other.
64. If any one destroy (another's) organ of generation, let him pay with *three leud-gelds* (*wergild* for manslaughter); if he pierce it through, let him make *bot* with six shillings; if it be pierced within, let him make *bot* with six shillings.
82. If a man carry off a maiden by force, let him pay fifty shillings to the owner, and afterwards buy (the object of) his will of the owner.

These laws provide us proof that slaves and even classes of slaves that we know almost nothing about existed in England.

Once large areas had been cleared of the native Britons, the invaders who had first come in scattered family groups began warring amongst themselves. This fiercely competitive Anglo, Saxon, and Jute intertribal conflict created another fresh source for slaves. For the victors, slaves were put work or sold for profit. One could obtain slaves from raiding and intertribal warfare however a financially destitute father might legally sell his children into slavery. The Church during and after that era had no qualms with the slavery practice and early English law provided that a priest who killed a man would lose his slaves. Abbots at Glastonbury possessed 108 slaves in 1086 A.D., 20 years after the Norman invasion. The Westminster Council did outlaw the sale of men in 1102 A.D., though what seems to have bothered the council more than anything else was the sale of *Aenglish* slaves into pagan countries where their souls were beyond the Church's reach.

No Euro-Christian group truly spoke out against the immorality of slavery until German Mennonites did so in the 1600's. Such trading continued as a black-market enterprise well into the 12th century. Ireland's port cities became a hub where many cultures came together to trade in human cargo.

Original tribal groups had four major divisions of social stratification, ranking individuals either as royalty, war leaders, common folk or slaves. The commoners provided their local royalty with food, shelter, service, and labor. The warrior leaders had distinguished themselves in battle. Royal bloodlines were believed to descend directly from *Woden*, a once-widespread cultural precept, as documented in the *Anglo-Saxon Chronicles*. Today's English royalty has its roots in those beliefs.

The value of a human being was expressed as the *wergild* paid to the kin of those individuals killed outside the parameters of war. A male commoner was "worth" about 200 shillings, a royal 1,200 shillings. These fees were levied at the *moot*, a court of commoners, which met every moon cycle at a specified place. The elite had representatives at these gatherings, but they did not control them, allowing respected commoners to administer the justice. Meetings convened at a sacred hill or tree with a "mark" as its border. If a *wergild* was not settled, the families involved sought blood reparation, the feud.

Anglo-Saxon Warrior Princes

Each early *Aenglish* region had its own royalty (descendants of *Woden*). These different regional princes were regularly struggling for dominance. Males in this position of influence rarely traveled without bodyguards close at hand. These princes had followers known as retainers. Such men were attracted to a prince by his reputation as a powerful warrior. Constant violent conquest kept the retainers and their prince supplied with food and post-combat celebrations. *Tacitus* noted on a visit to Germany that these fellows were not interested in gain by work but preferred continual warfare. Can you imagine what it would be like to live with groups like these roaming the countryside? Here are *Tacitus'* observations about these princes and their retainers:

> "The Princes fight for victory; for the Prince his followers fight. Many of the nobility, when their community comes to languish in its vigor by long peace and inactivity, betake themselves through impatience in other States which then prove to be in war. For, besides that this people cannot brook repose, besides that by perilous adventures they more quickly blazon their fame, they cannot otherwise than by violence and war support their huge train of retainers. For from the liberality of their Prince, they demand and enjoy that war-horse of theirs, with that victorious javelin dyed in the blood of their enemies. In the place of pay, they are supplied with a daily table and repasts; though grossly prepared, yet very profuse. For

maintaining such liberality and munificence, a fund is furnished by continual wars and plunder. Nor could you so easily persuade them to cultivate the ground, or to await the return of the seasons and produce of the year, as to provoke the foe and to risk wounds and death: since stupid and spiritless they account it, to acquire by their sweat what they can gain by their blood."

Sir Stenton wrote about this same topic:

"Everywhere in the Germanic world the ruler, whether king or chief, was attended by a body-guard of well-born companions. No Germanic institution has a longer history . . . The sanctity of the bond between lord and man, the duty of defending him and avenging a lord, the disgrace of surviving him . . . it was the personal reputation of a king which attracted retainers to his court, and it was the king's military household around which all early fighting centered . . . There is no essential difference between the king's companions of the heathen age and the nobles who attest the earliest English royal charters. . . . Unlike Gaul, Spain, and Italy, Britain was invaded not by tribes under tribal kings, but by bodies of adventurers, who according to their own traditions were drawn from three distinct Germanic peoples. Most of them came from remoter parts of the Germanic world, where kingship was less a matter of political authority than of descent from ancient gods. Respect for such descent, and the religion with which it was associated, survived even a migration across the North Sea, and meant any leader who could claim this divine ancestry might hope to establish himself as the king of some portion of the nation to which he belonged."

This is the cultural root of the warrior-king—a human being raised with the belief his lineage justified his exploits.

He attracted retainers that would rather fight than work for a living. These middlemen, who became the lords, also required a lavish life style provided by the work and food rent of the so-called lower classes. Thus was born the *Aenglish* system of taxation.

During the early *Aenglish* settlement of the Britons' isle, a common born freeman attained a *hide*, or tract of land to farm. From his crop and other labors he was expected to contribute a certain amount to support the royalty, which was then combined with the production of a number of other *hides* probably cultivated by the region of related kin groups. The demands of *Offa* an early royal, one of the major heroes in Germanic legend, whose great-grandson *Icel* founded the *Mercian* dynasty in 8th Century England, is evidence of this early taxation. "Sixty *hides* at Westbury on Trym were required to supply *King Offa*," wrote Stenton. This amounted to "two tuns full of clear ale, one 'cumb' full of mild ale, one 'cumb' full of British ale, seven oxen, six wethers, forty cheeses and thirty 'ambers' of meal."

The Anglo-Saxons brought their social structure with them to their new island home. The family groups were known as *regio*, or regions, kinships comprised of freemen on land not owned by a lord or royalty. The freemen of the region were responsible together as a unit to pay the local kings food-rent. Here is where my ancestors come into view. Sir Stenton stated:

> No other example of the primitive West-Saxon shires show clear traces of an earlier and more popular organization of local government. . . . 'Wiltshire', which means the district dependent on Wilton, has replaced an earlier Wilsaetan, which simply meant 'the people by the river Wylye'. (Willies ton)

Freemen Become Subjects Of Centralized Monarchy

These separate entities either banded together to fight or fought individually among themselves until the 9th Century, when a few larger kingdoms remained rather than a vast number of smaller fiefdoms. The survivors divided themselves into separate shires, each under the control of a centralized ruler— a long transition began from the status of freeman to subject, resulting from tribal aggression between different competitive groups of Angles or Saxons. In the earliest Anglo-Saxon laws freeman are written of, but by the time of *Aelfred* around 900 A.D. there is no mention of freemen in his laws, only kings and lords. This evolution directly translated into the consolidation of power wielded by a single privileged class, the direct descendants of *Woden* (*Votawn*, Odin) and their retainers.

Eventually, the royal bureaucracy greatly expanded so that those below lord status lost even their freedom to roam and own land. By 1066 A.D. all the land was owned by royalty or the church and everyone worked for someone else all the way up through nobles and the king. Not only were commoners forced to till the soil and labor to build grand houses for their masters, but they were conscripted to fight in wars to keep those same men in power, laying down their very lives to support the idea that some men are born as direct children of God to be rulers over other men.

The Danish Vikings invaded the island in 830 A.D. They established a fortified village (military base) and could not be dislodged. From there they worked outward plundering the countryside. Alfred a royal Saxon, who had his name spelled *AELFRED* on the *Aelfred* jewel, united the 9th Century Angles and Saxons to resist the new invaders. He also began an early arms race to beat the Danish attempting to gain control of the island. He sought the advantage by building longer boats. For the speed of boats with displacement hulls (all early boats) correlates directly to length, and in them his warriors were able to chase down the Danish raiders at sea.

Besides centralizing the power of one monarch, *Aelfred* known as the Great accomplished many things including defeating the Danish. *Aelfred* managed to push the Danish back offshore by building a centralized government of the people. He is credited with popularizing our written language and commissioning the *Anglo-Saxon Chronicles*. He learned Latin and traveled twice to Rome in his youth. These journeys marked the beginnings of a strong royal tie to Christendom that would figure heavily in the course of both English and American history.

In the winter of 1066 A.D., *King Eadward the Confessor* fell comatose for an extended time. When he suddenly awoke he called his advisors to him, claiming he'd had a vision of long-dead saints. These saints told him devils were coming to the island to burn and kill because of English sins. He named *Harold Godwain* to succeed him, *Godwain* was of common bloodline, and then *Eadward* died. The *witan* approved of the choice but other relatives of *Eadward* felt differently.

William of Normandy waited across the cold channel. Another tribe of Vikings related to the Anglo-Saxons who conquered Britain had settled along some of the coastal regions of France. William was a French-speaking cousin to *Eadward*. He had told everyone he was going to be the next English monarch. When the old sovereign died and *Godwain* was named king, William was livid. Scarcely ten months after *Godwain's* ascension to the English throne, William led an assembled group of continental knights across the water, hoping for riches and glory. After his group of mercenaries gathered for the trip they waited six weeks for a south wind to come and carry them across the Channel. They could only sail before the wind in those times. This wait ended up serving them well.

On that prevailing north wind came *King Harald* of Norway and the new *Aenglish King Godwain's* brother *Tostig*, an earl who'd been exiled for his cruelty by *Eadward*. This attack was turned back on September 25th at Stamford Bridge in northern England. It had been a very hard fight with many losses and left the *Aenglish* resistance weakened. *Godwain* and his men were still in the north when William landed in the south.

Before William set sail he had been able to negotiate the blessings of the Pope on his mission against the *Aenglish* monarch. From this barter he gained the privilege of carrying the Pope's banner, the Pope's seal on his ring, and around his neck a small locket that held some bones of a saint. This papal blessing was very disheartening to the *Aenglish* serving under *Godwain*. The *Aenglish* sent money to the Church in Rome and believed the Pope represented God on Earth. According to their belief, if one should die fighting the Pope's agent, that fighter would go to hell.

The bloody battles that followed William's invasion featured a blocking attempt by the *Aenglish* at Hastings to close off William's path inland. William and his continental knights repeatedly charged while their resisters hacked at them with two-handed axes or defended themselves with spears. William also had archers with him who continually rained down arrows upon *Godwain's* army. No archers supported the *Aenglish* ranks of that era because the bow was considered a weapon used by commoners for poaching deer. Only nobles could rightfully possess and use the bow because only they had the right to kill deer. The Anglo-Saxon *thanes* who were enlisted at their *Aenglish* lords' command fought without heavy horses, stood and repulsed charge after charge by William's mounted army from mid-morning until late in the day, when the banner of their last Saxon king fell. With nightfall the survivors made their way to the woods, fleeing to safety just as the Welsh had done many hundred years before, when Germanic invaders defeated the original Britons.

William's troops plundered and raped the *Aenglish* for months thereafter cutting a circle 20 miles outward from London. As William was being crowned in London, his men were setting fire to the city. The new monarch effectively established his rule with the backing of the Roman Church authority. French-speaking nobles moved in to administrate over the land they now controlled, each conscripting *Aenglish* common folk to build lavish castles such as those favored in France. Many uprisings followed that were violently put down. The so-called Norman Yoke settled quickly on *Aenglish* shoulders and was never dislodged. Any resistance was quelled swiftly and brutally.

The new ruling class spoke a different language. But, warfare and class structure remained a foundation of daily life. William, the new monarch, organized the *Doomsday Book* as an inventory of the properties to be taxed in the part of England he controlled. Subsequently, taxation became even more highly organized, and served to further entrench the elite in their lavish lifestyle. Their divine privilege was serving them well. It is an idea that still lives on today. The notion that one bloodline was favored by God above all others does not die easily. Just past the title page in my grandfather's King James Bible these words are printed:

> "To the most high and mighty Prince JAMES by the grace of God King of Great Britain, France, and Ireland,

defender of the faith, etc. the Translators of the Bible wish Grace, Mercy, and Peace, through Jesus Christ our Lord. Great and manifold were the blessings, most dread Sovereign, which almighty God, the Father of all mercies, bestowed upon us the people of England, when first he sent Your Majesty's Royal Person to rule and reign over us."

Such a flattering dedication is not surprising: James paid for the Biblical translation. It is important to note King James was the last king to insist upon the divine rights of the monarch. He lost his long and bloody struggle for this idea of divine right to the people of England, who officially put his claim to rest. But his outlook was rooted in a long history of divine privilege, the remains of which may still be seen today.

These are the roots of our class system and the individualist, freedom-loving freeman warrior-competitive culture. The cultural roots support the privileges and hoards of a select few supported by the work of many, in effect using human beings as slaves. It is accepted and desired by many within our culture to control or hoard great wealth, as long as it is done within a (relative) current legal framework.

This model is not the only way people live. It is only what we have been taught to accept as *normal* through many generations of culture. There are other, far more cooperative cultures and voices that might teach us about living healthy with compassion for each other. But if we forever judge these meeker cultures by these ancient Viking values of wealth accumulation or ability to produce and use quality weapons, we will never hear these less violent cooperative voices telling us about their own truly legitimate ways to live on Earth. Our ancient story will just repeat the past with new chapters written, based upon the old theme. And, indeed it is doing just that.

3

The Aenglish
Come To America

Ap		pproximately 1,000 years after the birth of Christ, the average *Aenglish* freeman did not own land. Instead it belonged to nobility or the Church, and he merely labored in the manner of lifelong indentured servitude. This loss of personal freedom for the common people began about the time of the original Saxon landing; but a resistive struggle for greater self-determination continued until a number of these commoners left the island, seeking greater personal freedoms. The earliest did so because of disagreements with the powers of the Church and king.

The Anglican Church became a powerful entity through the Middle Ages connected directly to the King of England. Different *Aenglish* monarchs had varying degrees of interaction with the church, but each king or queen appointed the Archbishop of Canterbury, who in effect became a kind of British Pope controlling the church in England. The Archbishop and his subordinates held their positions at the pleasure of the king, depending upon royal authority to maintain large estates worked by lessers and slaves. Thus the higher bishops and their consorts had good reason for declaring to the people that their kings were men sent by God to rule Great Britain. Though the Bible became the backbone of the English church, very few *Aenglish* people could read it because it was commonly written in Latin in those times. When universities came into being at Oxford and Cambridge, scholars such as John Wycliffe began to translate the book to English for the first time, from its Greek and Latin forms. These university scholars were not a formal part of the religious establishment, and their effort was in the beginning violently opposed by King Henry VIII and his Archbishop of York, Thomas Wolsey.

The English Translation Of The Bible Becomes A Source Of Revolution

William Tyndale was one of the first to make his early translation available to the public. His New Testament appeared in 1526 and the Bible in its entirety by 1535. His simple prose set the standard style for later English translations. William had to do this translation secretly in Germany while hiding from the *English* king. There he met and found the support of the controversial reformer Martin Luther, who was also translating the scriptures into his native German. Back in old *England*, Archbishop Wolsey burned these first "heretic" texts. The king sent agents to Germany in order to find Tyndale. When they found him in Antwerp he was imprisoned for a year and four months before being strangled and burned at the stake. His last reputed words were "Lord may you open the eyes of the king!" Ironically, the work of Tyndale and Wycliffe before him would form the foundation of King James's authorized version of 1611.

The previous development of the printing press by Gutenberg and others in Germany allowed for quick circulation of the book in England. Copies fairly poured in, with a result that was similar to the later appearance of television in the middle of the 20th Century—everybody had to have one. The ability to read and study the Bible in English sparked personal interpretations apart from doctrine and led to new social discontent. When the Anglo-Saxon working folk read the Bible they discovered that they were all related through Adam and Eve. There were no noble lords and ladies, or kings descended directly from *Woden*. People began to tire of oppression by the king and his bishops, comparing their ruler's opulent lifestyle with their own poorer circumstances.

The English Protestant movement formed during this period of Bible-based upheaval amid dissatisfaction with the old social conditions. Some sought to reform the extravagant ways of the King's church, naming themselves Puritans to signify their efforts to purify the British church. A different group and separatist faction—also called Brownists, in honor of their leader Robert Brown—advocated breaking away from the Anglican Church's control in favor of local control for individual congregations. Puritans proper were more moderate with their approach. They sought a central path between the rigid Roman Catholic type of ceremony and elaborate vestments and the outright breaking up of the Church. They rejected the finery and lavish lifestyle of the privileged class, choosing to wear plain clothes and spurn jewelry or other ornamentation. They vocally resisted what they viewed as corrupt and would not swear oaths.

Noble families and royalty still believed that they were accorded special favor from God. They worked to retain control of the common people and the religious establishment supported the royalty. Henry VIII had officially broken with the Roman Catholic Church, largely because it would not support his divorce from his wife. The rulers of the Elizabethan era continued to perpetuate the Protestant outlook. Elizabeth I continued the royal control of the church's front office. The Virgin Queen was a social and political powerhouse, largely due to both her tough personality and the fact that she surrounded herself with able advisors.

James Stuart had stronger notions when he assumed the English throne upon the death of his childless Tudor cousin Elizabeth. James was a preacher of the Divine Right of the Monarchy.

"As it is atheism and blasphemy to dispute what God can do," said James, "so it is presumption and a high contempt in a subject to dispute what a King can do, or say that a King cannot do this or that." His notion of *The True Law of Free Monarchy* held that, ". . . although a good King will frame his actions to be according to law, yet he is not bound thereto, but of his own will."

James' idea of sovereignty placed him above legal reproach. His contempt for Parliament and battles with this legislative body shaped his reign and legacy. The doctrine of a divinely bestowed authority was preached from the pulpit. Clergymen of that era were quick to stroke the hand of power, teaching that passive obedience to the monarch was a religious obligation. When James first ascended the throne, 800 Puritan churchmen petitioned him to leave the religious structure in place, but reform its courts, books, and seminary training while enforcing a more strict observance of the Sabbath. In turn he ridiculed them and their *Millenary Petition*. The English historian Green wrote that the Anglican bishops had, ". . . declared the insults he showered on their opponents were dictated by the Holy Ghost." Even so, there were those who dared to dispute the king's infallibility. He broke apart the conference with a threat that neatly summed up his policy: "I will make them conform, or I will harry them out of the land." We must remember that James was the patron of the King James version of the Bible. The bonded power of church and state led to social upheaval when James dissolved Parliament for a seven-year stretch, begetting a rash of civil discontent and emigration from the island.

The next king, Charles I held his father's views on the issue of God-given authority. When he took over in 1625 matters worsened, Charles I was aided by men like William Laud, Archbishop of Canterbury, who resisted any change to old customs and sought to purge the Anglican Church of its Puritan sect.

The group of Brownists Separatist Protestants who boarded the Mayflower held beliefs identified today as those of the most extreme members of this sect. Their actions were in direct resistance to the king's church. They believed in the right of the individual congregation, and became known as Congregationalists. This group had been living in exile in Leiden, the Netherlands for ten years under the leadership of William Brewster. Their expedition to the American continent was financed partly by London investors who were promised New World goods in exchange for their backing.

The Brownists landed in Massachusetts in 1620, the first of many settlers who would follow. Between 1629 and 1641 more than 20,000 people made the same migration, escaping conditions in England they felt were intolerable. These were the "eleven years' tyranny" pointed to by historians as the period Charles tried to rule his country without the voice of Parliament. In England, it was an era of legendary economic depression, disease, and migration.

The New American Theocracy

Those who fled sought America as a place to form a more perfect society, guided by the framework of their thoughts on freedom and religion. These people brought the seeds of our dominant cultural worldview to this continent from England. It is the roots of our American culture. It is our shared cultural inheritance, whether those of us living in America are in actuality of African or Irish or Indonesian or of any other ethnic descent. At this turning point in the story of America these families found themselves poised to alter the lives of every native soul inhabiting this continent.

The new society established in Massachusetts was a fundamental Puritan theocracy. If you were a man and a member of the church you could participate in the government that made and enforced the laws in this new place. If, on the other hand, you subscribed to the doctrine of the Quakers, you could be dragged from town to town and horsewhipped as a display of your sinful nature. John Endecott led 60 settlers to form the town of Salem in 1628, where he quickly acquired a reputation for general intolerance of religious dissenters. He showed particular cruelty to the Quakers or the Society of Friends, members of which he imprisoned, banished or executed. He also advocated the bloody 1636 strike against the native *Pequots*. In 1658 the "United Colonies of New England" elected him President, charging him with assuring mutual defense and safeguarding their religious values.

While these immigrants had fled an intolerant world, it is nevertheless this judgmental facet of English culture that they brought with them. This fundamentalist conservative and judgmental nature exists today in our culture much more dominant here than in any other country in the English-speaking world. Do we owe this to the great migration of these early Puritan settlers and others who followed them from England?

When these Protestant emigrants reached these shores they met darker skinned, scantily clad people who had never heard of Jesus Christ. Indigenous tribes in that part of the continent included the *Nipmuck*, the *Narragansett*, the *Pequot*, the *Pocumtuck*, and the *Wampanoag*. These were the people who lived inland and along the Massachusetts coast. A scouting party from the Mayflower encountered a group of unidentified natives, an incident that resulted in no casualties but left the tribesmen with a definite first impression of muskets and metal upper body armor. The foremost *Sachem* or chieftain of the *Wampanoags* at that time was *Massasoit*, a man who took pity on the suffering he witnessed that first winter. He made a peace agreement with Plymouth Colony. *Massasoit* remained true to his alliance with the settlers throughout the last forty years of his life. However, there were growing problems that developed in the aftermath of this first culture clash.

Aenglish Start To Show Their Violent Viking Ways In This Country

In the year after the Mayflower's voyage, another group of new arrivals established their own settlement at Weymouth. The Boston historian George Bodge recorded that "These colonists proved to be an indolent and wayward set, abused the confidence of the Indians, and finally caused a threatened outbreak." *Massasoit* sent a message to Governor Carver at Plymouth by way of a runner, *Hobomak*. After the Governor heard from the messenger, he sent Captain Miles Standish with eight military men to Weymouth to investigate the disagreement. This first military contact between the Separatists and the original inhabitants of Massachusetts ended in typical *Aenglish* Viking style: at least four dead natives, one of whom was decapitated. The head was fixed atop the blockhouse barricade to terrorize the local natives brutally warning them to beware. There was no major violent interaction again until after *Massasoit* died and his son *Metacom*, who was called King Philip by the Pilgrims, became chieftain.

Back home in England other Puritan leaders were negotiating an accord with King Charles. It became the Cambridge Agreement, which was signed in 1629 and formed the basis for the Massachusetts Bay Company. The next year they sailed with 17 ships under the command of John Winthrop. They joined Endecott's faction in Salem, before moving on to found Boston at the mouth of the Charles River. This group, mostly middle class could afford the expensive trip. Three-quarters of the people who made the voyage came in whole family groups paying between 50 and 80 English pounds depending on the size of the family. This was at a time when an English farmer made about 20 pounds a year. The heads of these families tended to be literate, skilled tradesmen of urban origin—only one-third were farmers, the rest city folk. The more agrarian among them found fertile river valleys receptive to the European plow, and began almost at once to turn out good crops of flax and hemp for cloth. There were many weavers among them.

When a group of hereditary aristocrats in England in-

quired about coming to Massachusetts, they were told their social station would not be recognized in the new colony. Even
so, Fischer described how this smaller slice of society became
an American system of rank based on the status of "lesser gen-
try, yeomanry and cottagers." Strict rules of social deference
dominated all interaction between people. Those born of lower
rank were expected to bow or curtsy to their social superiors,
even when passing one another on a public roadway. Travelers
visiting as late as the 19th Century expressed astonishment at
the sight of New England schoolchildren bowing to their "bet-
ters" at the edge of a cart path.

The society they constructed was a very rigid reflection of
their religious beliefs. All matters pertaining to dress, recre-
ation, music, commerce and social standing were rigidly prescribed and closely monitored by the church elders and
magistrates. Cosmetics were condemned. Women were summoned into court over the amount of lace and ribbon they
wore. Athletic endeavors believed "unwarranted" were sup-
pressed in the sternest terms, and playing any sports on Sun-
days was actively punished. Thrift and industry were
encouraged as a part of the very fabric of moral virtue.

These early American leaders believed that an individual
must personally read the Bible to have a chance at salvation.
They held the hard-line Calvinist attitude that entrance into
heaven was predestined, determined before birth by God. God
had chosen his elect.

Some of the new arrivals felt the native people might also
enter heaven if they were able to read the Bible or hear the
word. The seal of the new colony depicted a drawing of a native woman and the words, "Come over and help us." Money
was raised for that purpose just in case the native souls were
predetermined to be acceptable to God. Efforts began to con-

vert the native people to read the Scriptures, pray to the one God, and attend Protestant church services with the same piety practiced by the Puritans. The English perceived Indian cooperation in these matters as a sign that the heathen had good intentions and it was rewarded.

John Eliot printed 2,000 Bibles in translations of English written syllables of the *Algonquin* spoken language. However, very few native people could read English. Native Americans who understood and could read English were not trusted, making conversion to Christianity difficult. All of that meant little to the Puritans. Attempts to share the Gospel with the natives may have been a genuine mark of goodwill in the hearts of some, most *Aenglish* considered the tribal folk to be heathens at best, barely human if at all, without claim to privileges accorded as the natural birthright of Englishmen in any class. For mainstream church and political figures this was not even open to debate. In 1906 Bodge wrote:

> "It is enough to say here that the government of the country followed their course of settlement with small regard to the rights of the natives. In some of the plantations, the settlers purchased their lands of the Indians, as a matter of precaution; partly that they might have to show [a] title in case any other claim should be set up in opposition to theirs, and partly to conciliate the savages, whose hostility they feared, and whose friendship was profitable in the way of trade, in furs and other products of the hunt. The English paid no heed to Indian laws or customs and religious ideas, with no apparent thought of their intolerance and injustice. They made out deeds, in language only the learned framers themselves could understand."

As related by historian Jill Lepore in her book, *The Name of War, King Philip's War and the Origins of the American*

Identity, John Winthrop argued that only when land was fenced, tilled and built-upon could it be owned, and therefore the native people could not own any, "for they inclose no ground, neither have they cattell to maintayne it, but remove their dwellings as they have occasion." The newcomers might then, by the letter of their own law, claim land simply by squatting and "improving" it, without regard to the seasonal migrating natives.

Local tribes of varying disposition reacted differently to this typical, contemptuous entrance by the Saxon descendents. Directly west of Boston dwelled the *Nipmuck*, while Plymouth was *Wampanoag* country. The *Narragansett* lived in Rhode Island and the *Pocumtuck* hunted over more mountainous terrain on the western side of Massachusetts. In Connecticut were the *Mohegan* and *Pequot* people, also called *Pequod* in some accounts. Either spelling is a derivation of an *Algonquin* word for "destroyer," applied to them because of how they moved into that part of the country. They looked least kindly on the *Aenglish* presence. The *Pequot* were trading partners of the Dutch in New York. Before the first colonies were founded, in fact, the *Pequot* came down through the Connecticut River valley to forcefully displace its prior inhabitants. This tribe's aggressiveness made it an important ally or feared enemy, whichever way the perspective fell.

By the 1630s Dutch traders had established trading posts south of the primary Puritan bases in what is now New York. A cultural upheaval ensued when European trade goods were bartered with the natives especially guns and alcohol. The Dutch and the English vied to profit from the native trade, playing the tribes against one another. Such a loyalty tug-of-war effectively split the *Pequot* tribal group, a split that saw some side with the *Mohegan* and British and others with the

Dutch. It must be noted that most of the history from this period poured from English pens but what is clear is that native politics played heavily in the building of new alliances. The *Narragansett* did not like the *Pequot* who were allied to the Dutch, so they made an agreement with the English.

In 1634 a Captain John Stone of the West Indies sailed his ship up the Connecticut River on a trip to reach New Amsterdam (New York City) from Boston. This man's reputation was little better than that of a pirate, but the Puritans would soon be granting him the nobility of a martyr. He and his crew were slain en route by what was presumably a Dutch-favoring *Pequot* group. Soon thereafter, an English-minded group of the same tribe sent messengers to the Massachusetts Bay Colony to sue for friendship and trading rights. The colonials accused this *Pequot* group of Stone's murder. The magistrate demanded that those individuals who killed the trader be handed over for prosecution. Needless to say, this wasn't going to happen. An uneasy truce was reached after the *Pequot* presented many pelts and beaver furs.

The next year a hot-headed adventurer named John Oldham, a person the historian Howard Zinn identified as an "Indian-kidnaper and troublemaker," was on a trading run near Block Island when he and his crew were surprised and killed by a group of local natives. A Boston sailor, John Gallop, came upon the scene of the crime and tried to hail any survivors. He saw only a few natives unsuccessfully attempting to sail away in the vessel. Gallop and his sons fired on the Indians, who ran below decks before being boarded. Gallop found Oldham dead, wrapped up in his fishing nets. The sailors killed one native and captured a second, while several others escaped. Gallop tried to tow the boat to Saybrook Fort but had to eventually cut it adrift because of heavy seas.

The two tribesmen who escaped had originally been part of Oldham's crew, and had no part in the murders. They told *Canonicus, Sachem* of the *Narragansett* there, about the events that occurred on Oldham's boat. This chieftain sent a message to Governor Winthrop through Roger Williams, of Providence, whom they trusted, stating that he *Canonicus* had sent a strong force to Block Island to seek out the men who did the deed. In response the Massachusetts magistrates sent a party to *Canonicus* demanding the return of stolen property and vengeance upon the murderers. Gallop's prisoner, in the meantime, had escaped and sought refuge among the *Pequot*.

Genocidal Wars Begin In Massachusetts

Bodge and Zinn related that Winthrop, not satisfied to wait, lost little time dispatching his own military force to Block Island. True to their heritage, all 90 English fighters volunteered. They were ordered to seize the whole island and put its entire male population to death (while at the same time the orders stated that the condemned somehow pay restitution via "one thousand fathom of *wampom*"). The children of the island were to become hostages. With this task complete they were to visit similar justice upon the *Pequot* camps.

On the last day of August 1636, these citizen soldiers closed in on Block Island and met a hail of arrows. They had body armor and helmets that protected them. Only two were wounded, while the return musket fire they gave drove the archers into the woods. The *Aenglish* burned two separate villages and many acres of native corn. Unable to find any people, they returned to their boats and set off to find the *Pequot*. At Saybrook Fort twenty more men joined their cause, as well as two interpreters including a young *Wampanoag* called John

Sassomon. At an inlet near the first *Pequot* village, an inhabitant approached them in a dugout canoe and asked what they wanted. Captain John Underhill told this man that they came on the Governor's business to speak with the *Sachems*. The *Aenglish* were told that the leader *Sassacus* was on a trip to Long Island, so Underhill demanded that other *Sachems* come out to meet them.

When they went ashore 300 warriors met them, but no *Sachems*. The captain stated his terms in a brief, confrontational meeting, immediately demanding the murderers and payment for damages. Predictably, the warriors did not comply, even assuming they had a decent understanding of what their visitors meant. The iron guns going off scattered them as it had the Block Island villagers. Again the *Aenglish* iron body armor protected them from the arrows and the citizen-soldiers put the encampment to the torch, though the corn there was too green to burn. They headed back to Boston having effectively declared war through these actions.

Pequot retaliation was swift and decisive. Outposts along the Connecticut River took the first blows, and Saybrook Fort was besieged for a matter of months. Pilgrims at Plymouth wrote a complaint to the Massachusetts Bay Colony for the reaction Winthrop had initiated. In 1637 nine Englishmen and three women were killed in Connecticut, one of the men tortured to death. Two little girls were captured but later recovered. A score of men went to Saybrook's aid while the other colonies raised an army numbering 160 men under Captain Israel Stoughton of Dorchester. Plymouth Colony sent 50 men in non-combatant roles, though the 90 men from the Connecticut River valley who mustered under the leadership of Windsor's John Mason did so solely to launch an offensive effort.

Seventy *Mohegan* joined their ranks even before the Massachusetts forces arrived.

The newly formed army first came to a pair of *Pequot* villages with well-defended palisades making conquest difficult. So the English went off to solicit the *Narragansett* for aid on this mission. They played on the hatred between the tribes to their advantage, and requested a show of support as proof of sincere friendship. A few hundred warriors reluctantly went along. In the *Pequot* villages the *Sachem Sassacus* believed the English had returned to Hartford, and went after them there with a large war party. But the colonial army seeking help from the *Narragansett* had gone along a different path. They eventually returned to the *Pequot* village near present-day Groton in the early morning on May 26th. Nearly all the warriors had gone with *Sassacus*, leaving the elderly or infirm with women and children inside the wooden-walled fortification. The *Narragansett* hung back as the English divided into three units to circle the camp under the poor early light. At dawn they poured the first round of musket blasts through the perimeter.

Though the *Aenglish* attackers had previously reached an agreement not to immediately set fire to the town in order to preserve as much plunder as possible, it wasn't long before the town was in flames. Estimates vary considerably, but within an hour's time the 90 Englishmen under Mason managed to shoot or burn to death between 400–700 villagers, mostly women and children. Only seven escaped death and those survivors were taken away as prisoners. Such ferocity shocked the *Narragansett*. Lepore stated that they refused to participate in the slaughter, crying "*Mach it! Mach it!*" (That is: *It is too much!*). During this slaughter, warriors in the second *Pequot* village detected smoke rising from the first. The sound of their war cries could be heard as they approached the village arriving at approximately the same time as a group of European reinforcements commanded by one Captain Patrick. The enraged warriors fiercely attacked and pushed the English into slow retreat back towards the Mystic River. Eventually, the harassed English found safety behind walls of Saybrook fort. The *Narragansett* were sent home with the *Aenglish* wounded.

Even as they mourned, the surviving *Pequot* resolved to burn their other village and all the possessions they could not carry before splitting up their tribe. Some made for Long Island and seeking what protection might be found with the Dutch. The English sent out native scouts to track their flight. Captain Stoughton arrived at Saybrook with his group of 120 men. The combined forces marched twelve miles upriver to capture a *Pequot* band splintered from the rest. The native people gave up without resistance. The English took 22 of the men out in Gallop's boat beyond the harbor and executed them. Two were spared on the condition that they lead the English to *Sassacus*. Bodge noted that of the 80 women and children, 33 were given to the Mohegan and the rest sent to Boston, where they were sold into slavery.

In his progress-report to Governor Winthrop, Captain Stoughton wrote:

". . . you shall receive forty-eight or fifty women and children, unless there stay any here to be helpful, etc., concerning which there is one, that is the fairest and largest that I saw amongst them, to whom I have given a coat to cloathe her. It is my desire to have her for a servant, if it may stand with your good liking, otherwise not. There is a little squaw that Steward Culacut desireth, to whom he hath given a coate. Lieut. Davenport desireth one, to wit, a small one. Sosomon, the Indian, desireth a young little squaw, which I know not."

The two captives guided the English to a swampy area near what is now Fairfield, Connecticut where a large group of the remaining *Pequot* had found refuge with a friendly tribe. At their approach all the natives took cover in the marsh, which the attackers surrounded. When their captives told the English that the Indians had 16 guns in their possession, they were more willing to negotiate. One of them, Thomas Stanton, was fairly fluent in the *Pequot* tongue. He walked in and explained the terms, coming back with 200 natives who peacefully surrendered. These were the *Pequot* women and children and the members of the band they were visiting.

Those warriors who remained let it be known they intended to fight it out to the death. An hour before daybreak they massed in one area under *Sassacus* who Mason estimated still led about 70 men. The Indians were able to break through the English line but their flight didn't save them. When they tried to find safety with the *Mohawks*, that group of the Six Nations demonstrated their loyalty to the British by killing the escaped *Pequot* and sending the scalps to the English.

Of the 180 *Pequot* women and children survivors, most were divided between the Massachusetts and Connecticut fighters who used them as "servants." The Indians were treated as booty of war, much like those captives in earlier times when the Englishmen's ancestors worshipped *Woden* and Thor. Two women and 15 boys were sent to Bermuda to be sold in the slave markets there. Stoughton remained in the area until the end of summer, systematically destroying the native crops and winter food supply. On their way home Stoughton's men destroyed any rebuilt shelters and any other crops they found on Block Island.

The Puritans believed their victory was God-given. Such sentiments were documented in William Bradford's work, *History of the Plymouth Plantation*. Because of the high literacy rate among the colonists, there were many accounts written about the war with the *Pequot* people. These works were very biased against the Indians. The English writers believed obliterating the tribe was a positive accomplishment, beginning the American phase of the conquering warrior typified by their Anglo-Saxon ancestors' history of warfare and enslavement of the conquered. A formal 1638 treaty between the English, *Narragansett* and *Mohegan* indicated that the 200 or so surviving *Pequot* would be scattered, sold or taken as wives with the children adopted into other native groups.

The result of this first campaign unmistakably demonstrated an *Aenglish* willingness to take whatever measures necessary to gain what they desired. What they wanted was also painfully clear: the whole of this new land, which they found much more appealing than their old one. The Anglo-Saxons' abandonment of Germany in favor of the British Isle echoed violently here across the waters many years later.

As time passed, the native tribes desired more and more European trade goods. Trading with the newcomers changed the life of the native people and fostered dependence on the Europeans. North American native peoples had never worked metal, except for the hammering of copper. No longer totally self-sufficient, the native people wanted rifles for hunting and fighting, meaning they also required steady supplies of powder and lead ammunition. They also enjoyed the manufactured mirrors, blankets, better knives and iron cooking pots. The introduction of European liquor, addictive to many Indians unaccustomed to alcoholic beverages, altered many of their lives beyond repair.

In exchange for the right to trade, the English demanded loyalty from their customers. Religion formed an additional part of this cultural interaction. The emigrants pressured their clients to dress and worship as they did, treating such behavior as an indication that the tribes were setting aside heathen ways and false idols. They saw the hunter-gatherer lifestyle and lack of a written language as signs of heathenism. Not many Englishmen learned the native languages. They considered such dialects barbarous and even satanic although they retained many native names such as Massachusetts, among many, many others. Traders relied on interpreters, generally natives like John Sassomon, who was raised by colonists after his *Wampanoag* parents died of smallpox during his childhood.

Roger Williams is largely remembered for his democratic views. He riled many peers with the argument that the English ought to at least pay for native lands before taking possession of them, and was nearly deported for this idea. He also declared that church and government should be separate entities. He became an outcast because his radical ideas were unacceptable to the majority of the English so he started a settlement at Providence, Rhode Island. Williams promised that his new settlement would tolerate religious freedom and it became a safe haven for Quakers and other victims of the Pilgrims' religious intolerance. He worked closely with and lived among native tribal villagers, particularly the *Narragansett*. Williams' *A Key into the Language of America* (1643) was the first notably scientific attempt by one of the Europeans to accurately record the speech, customs and spiritual beliefs of the Native Americans. He wrote:

"They have no *Clothes, Bookes,* nor *Letters,* and conceive their *Fathers* never had; and therefore they are easily perswaded that the *God* that made *English* men is a greater *God,* because Hee hath so richly endowed the *English* above *themselves*: But when they heare that about sixteen hundred yeeres agoe, *England* and the *Inhabitants* thereof were like unto *themselves,* and since have received from *God, Clothes, Bookes,* &c. they are greatly affected with a secret hope concerning *themselves.*"

Whatever he decided, he held firm to his conviction that it was a sacred duty to bring "the mercies of *Europe*" to "these *Gentiles* of America;" he took great encouragement from the fact that some of their oral traditions concerned a figure named *Wetucks,* "a man that wrought great *Miracles* amongst them, and *walking upon the waters,* &c. with some kind of broken Resemblance to the *Sonne of God.*"

Massasoit the *Wampanoag Sachem* who had made and held the peace with the first Puritan settlers off the Mayflower, died in 1662. The elderly chief held fast to his agreement until the end of his life, despite colonial problems with other tribes. His hereditary position passed to his eldest son, *Wamsutta.* He died within a year. *Metacom* his younger brother then stepped into this leadership role. During their youth both brothers were given English names, Alexander and Philip. *Metacom* or Philip had signed a loyalty agreement with the English in 1662 although he could not read the document.

King Philip's Devastating War

When *Metacom* assumed the leadership of his tribe, John Sassomon returned to live in the main village and acted as *Meta-*

com's interpreter and scribe. The interpreter had studied at the newly established Harvard College (now University), and as such was a rare *Wampanoag* who could read and write English. Sassomon's loyalties seem to have been forever divided by his dual-citizenship in native and English worlds. *Metacom* was repeatedly swindled in land deals written and translated by Sassomon, who eventually left his position as translator and returned to the English. The English granted him a small place in a Christian native town, *Natik*, where he assumed the role of preacher.

As the English population grew, *Metacom's* patience wore thin as 20,000 colonists became 30,000, all wanting land, and pressuring the natives for cultural and religious conversion. Their livestock ruined *Wampanoag* crops and the population of wild game dwindled under the guns of the Europeans. These pressures and superior attitudes became too much for *Massasoit's* heir. He began to talk of rebellion and worked to unify the tribes around him to this cause.

Rhode Island Deputy Governor John Easton describes Philip's grievance as such: ". . . that they had a great fear to have any of their Indians called or forced to be Christian Indians. They said that such were in everything more mischievous, only dissemblers, and then the English made them not subject to their kings [chiefs], and by lying to wrong their kings."

Metacom's worries were justified and he began to envision a rebellion that would be an all-or-nothing struggle to push the colonials off the continent. John Sassomon became aware of these plans and went to the leadership of the Plymouth Colony in the dark of night. They summoned *Metacom* into court on charges that he was starting a rebellion. Nothing was conclusively proven against him with this trial, but *Metacom* learned the identity of his accuser. John Sassomon was discovered under the ice in a pond near his home during January of 1675. His gun and hat lay on the surface and no one knew what had happened to him. Later, a single questionable witness appeared to blame three prominent friends of the *Wampanoag* leader. Tried in Plymouth, these three were convicted and hanged by the English magistrates. This judgment served as the proverbial last straw.

Metacom stated that ". . . if twenty honest Indians testified that an Englishman had done them wrong, it was nothing, and if but one of the worst Indians testified against any Indian or their [chief] when it pleascd the English then that was sufficient." Though they had been warned about a possible uprising, most of the colonists apparently did not view the warning as a serious threat.

This naiveté ended on June 24th 1675, when hostile warriors began shooting a farmer's cattle outside Swansea, Massachusetts. In response the man shot and wounded one of the natives, after which they killed him and eight or ten others living there, and burned his homestead to the ground. What followed became known as King Philip's War and marked the bloodiest period in early Amcrican history, a clash for survival between two extremely different cultures. The desperate times led to atrocities committed by both sides. In this country in 2007 A.D. we cannot possibly comprehend such fury visited upon our own homes and communities. Experiencing and or witnessing brutality changes human beings.

Captain Samuel Mosely led a group of men called the "Bay Volunteers" from Boston. Mosely was a so-called *privateer*, or legalized pirate, and renowned for his fights with the Dutch. When the natives burned the first house at Swansea the war was on. It took Mosely and his volunteers only three days to arrive on the scene. He brought 90 men and many ferocious dogs.

These men and dogs reputedly did many brutal things during this fighting. My ancestor John Williston was with Mosely.

This was a long and desperate war the likes of which had not been encountered by the Europeans in their earlier struggles with the Indians. Many people were killed or brutalized on both sides. The taking of captives and acts of decapitation were commonplace. English soldiers piked the heads on poles for trophies, while native warriors hung them in trees as warnings. Many English hostages were taken and adopted into tribes to replace others who had perished. Colonists executed or sold their captives into slavery on Barbados plantations.

The dominant cultural attitude of the New England colonists toward the original inhabitants was one of superiority. They did not accept the native people as equals. The English had difficulty accepting the fact that the Native Americans already had sovereign nations of their own, each with legitimate social organization, ways of conduct, and territory. This ethnocentric attitude has survived to the present: Today our culture measures other races and nations around the globe, with our template or paradigm of living.

In 17th Century Massachusetts, the Puritans believed native peoples represented evil incarnate. The theologian Cotton Mather is a representative voice, much celebrated by his own culture for his scientific outlook and the first American born on this soil honored by induction into the Royal Society of London. Mather's views about the natives explicitly revealed the English opinion of their one-time hosts. Historian Lepore quoted Mathers:

> "These parts were covered with nations of barbarous Indians and infidels, in whom the prince of power of the air did work as a spirit: nor could it be expected that the na-

tions of wretches, whose whole religion was the most explicit sort of devil-worship, should not be acted by the devil to engage in some early and bloody action, for the extinction of a plantation so contrary to his interests, as that of New England . . ."

Lepore also cited John Richardson, who preached that ". . . war is an ordinance appointed by God for subduing and destroying the Church's Enemies here upon Earth." By murdering Indians the Puritans claimed to be acting as God's instruments, freeing the land from its "perfect children of the Devil." For many New Englanders, King Philip's War was thus a holy one; that is, a moral fight waged for their religious convictions and the survival of their church. Since the natives were infidels, ". . . *blud for blud shal bee ther portion Just.*"

The native people of New England viewed the world through their paradigm. They were much more individualistic than the Puritans were. Each tribal group followed its own inspiration and within groups each individual was free to follow or not follow the tribe. They accepted their leaders based upon personal choice. They were still freemen and women. Though these groups spoke related languages, each of the *Algonquin* tribes represented a very individual and separate entity. At times these groups cooperated with one another and at others they did not. They always remained independent.

When *Metacom* formed the resistance against the English, he did not realize the English strength of organization. He probably felt that each town was a separate tribe. The English, in his mind, would not pull together and unite against his tribe. While he may have envisioned taking 600 warriors from many tribes, moving from town to town, destroying each one-at-a-time, it seems he did not expect the English to be so organized in their own attacks and resistance against him. The English, in turn, feared *Metacom* would unite all the neighboring tribes under his leadership, though he was unable to accomplish this to that degree of unity.

Metacom's entire family was killed or captured, among them his wife and 9-year-old son. They and their living kin became part of the most profitable booty of the war, sold into slavery at two shillings apiece. When Indians began spreading their attacks to the edge of Virginia, plantation owners in Barbados feared word of it would lead to revolt among their holdings. Thus the governing body there (also English) passed a law to ban the purchase of native slaves in the islands. This ruined the New England slave business. Those native slaves en route were dumped overboard, or shipped to Tangiers, in Africa. Many Indians who sought amnesty, Christian or otherwise, met this fate. Only two colonists formally protested this practice of enslavement. John Eliot and William Leete, Deputy Governor of Connecticut wrote letters of complaint in 1675.

Christianized natives were sometimes passed over during this period of mayhem, identified by the towns where they lived or by the brass medallions they were given to wear around their necks to mark their Christianity. Natives who were spared death or enslavement were sent to places like Deer Island, near Boston, where half of them subsequently died of exposure or starvation. Compassionate men such as Eliot and an Irish immigrant, Daniel Gookin, tried to aid these unfortunates as best they could. For his troubles Gookin received death threats from fellow colonists.

The warfare continued and by July 22, 1676, Nathanial Saltonstall had exhaustively recorded that:

> "In Narragansett not one house left standing. At Warwick, but one. At Providence, not above three. At

Potuxit, none left. Very few at Seaconicke. At Sawnasey, two at most. Marlborough, wholly laid to ashes, except two or three houses. Grantham and Nashaway, all ruined but one house or two. Many houses burnt at Springfield, Scituate, Lancaster, Brookefield and Northhampton. The greatest part of Rehoboth and Taunton destroyed. Great spoil made at Hadley, Hatfield, and Chelmsford. Deerfield wholly, and Westfield much ruined. At Sudbury, many houses burnt, and some at Hingham, Weymouth, and Braintree. Besides particular farms and plantations, a great number not to be reckoned up, wholly laid to waste, or much damnified. And, as to persons, it is generally thought, that of the English there hath been lost, in all, Men, Women and Children, above eight hundred since the war began."

In August of the next year *Metacom* died, one of the last of his 3,000 tribesmen killed, shot by another Indian in league with the whites. The English surprised him near his ancestral home, a place ironically named Mount Hope. Commanding officer Benjamin Church stated that since the chief ". . . caused many an Englishman's body to be unburied, and to rot above the ground, not one of his bones should be buried." He pronounced the chief a "doleful, great, naked, dirty beast," and found an "old Indian executioner" to behead the corpse and quarter the body. The four parts were hung in different trees as a signal of final victory. On the 17th day of August, Benjamin Church marched to Plymouth, arriving just after the Reverend John Cotton finished his Thanksgiving sermon. The soldiers presented the townsfolk with the head of *Metacom*, whose father had celebrated the first Thanksgiving in Plymouth with refugees who sailed on the Mayflower some 55 years earlier. The round up and sale of native people as slaves did not stop with the death of *Metacom* but continued after the end of the rebellion.

Historians dwell on the *Wampanoag* uprising as a crucial episode in the English colonization of America. While other European nationalities were represented on this continent including the Dutch and Germans, they never experienced this type of rebellion. The warfare of the Indians against the English settlements, with the single-minded intent to drive the English back where they had come from did not occur on this kind of scale against the other Europeans. In fact most of them, including the French, who later made allies of the *Algonquin* tribes, had far better relations with the native peoples.

Why were the English so different?

The Germans and French, particularly, demonstrated a greater respect for the native people as human beings. Disrespect can be felt without verbal language. Disrespect is the fuel of social unrest. Lepore observed that, "The English typically considered Indians to be homeless nomads who could not own land since they did not 'improve' it, while at the same time believing those same Indians could legally sell their land to eager English purchasers."

The Pilgrims and those other Englishmen who came after them arrived in this country seeking freedom from persecution, and were accustomed to a feudal system in which they were essentially the property of a King or Lord. They were refugees of this system but brought it with them through their values and with their culture. With advanced weaponry and an attitude of superiority, the English were able to dominate another culture, displace the native people, and take them as slaves. This was the way the *Aenglish* had always known: the Viking way.

We are the inheritors of an *Aenglish* culture whose privileged forebears considered themselves direct descendents of *Woden*. We are people who have an exceptionally difficult time respecting the validity of other cultures unlike our own. Throughout our history, we have negated the rights of other cultures, not allowing them to exist in their own way and in their own place if they had something we wanted. If they are not warriors with equal weaponry, similar religions, similar colored skins we can more easily demonize them or discredit them for conquest. Today, we still call this continent's original folk by a name they received from a lost European merchant-explorer thinking he was somewhere else.

Can we wake up and change the future?

4

Ethnocentric Conquest

One hundred fifty years after the first Anglo-Saxon landing on the North American continent there were nearly 4 million English-speaking colonists living within 50 miles of the Atlantic Ocean. As the coastal *Aenglish* population expanded they began to move out across mountainous regions to the west, displacing natives. A similar pattern of events followed the conquest of Briton when Anglo-Saxons from Germany immigrated to the British Isle. From roughly 1790 to 1890, we expanded from sea to shining sea. Native peoples who survived the debilitating effects of European diseases and resisted this migration into their territory were killed or captured and marched west from their homelands to arid regions across the Mississippi River, into so-called Indian Territories. During this racial and cultural genocide, we made their religious practices illegal, forced their children into boarding schools where they were punished for speaking their own language, and tried to transform the rest of the native people into farmers in the *Aenglish* way.

War On The Haudenosaunee

At the time of our first contact with the native people the largest and most powerful organized group of Native Americans east of the Mississippi River were the *Iroquois* (*Haudenosaunee*) a united league of six nations. This league (at the time of the American Revolution) controlled an area from the Chesapeake Bay across Ohio into Kentucky to the junction of the Ohio and Mississippi Rivers up into all of southern Michigan and southern Ontario then back to both sides of the St. Lawrence River in New York State. At the beginning of the American Revolution the league council declared itself officially neutral and made efforts to stay that way. Professor Barbara Mann author of *George Washington's War on Native America* wrote:

> The Mohawk Sachem and Six Nations Speaker for the event, Tyorhansere ("Little Abraham"), remarked that, on "mature deliberation," it was "the determination of the Six Nations, not to take any part: but it is a family affair" between the British and the colonists, "to sit still and see you fight it out." Tyorhansere also requested that the Americans be sure of informing the entirety of the settlers of the arrangement so as "not to defile" the path between Philadelphia and Onondaga with blood, that is to prevent opportunistic raids on Iroquois by poorly informed settlers.

The attempted neutrality did not last. The *Oneida* and *Tuscarawa,* two of the six nations, sided with the American rebels. The *Cayuga, Mohawk, Onondaga* and *Seneca* pledged loyalty to the English representatives of King George. There had been a long tribal trading relationship with the English and that may have influenced this decision. The English also paid more for American scalps than frontier traders did for beaver pelts. This partnership with the English eventually caused the *Iroquois* to lose the greater part of their holdings south of Canada.

In the portion of George Washington's memoir concerning his early military career as the English king's representative from Virginia, he wrote about the *Seneca* Indians in Ohio who called him by another name. At the age of 21 in the middle of the winter of 1753, Washington traveled 250 miles from Williamsburg to Presque Isle near Lake Erie on a mission for the English colonial army. He met many native people on the way. In his own words:

> It was on this occasion he (GW) was named by the half-King (as he was called) and the tribes of Nations with whom he treated—Caunotaucarius (in English) the Town Taker; which name being registered in their Manner & communicated to other Nations of Indians, has been remembered by them ever since in all their transactions with him during the late war.

Professor Fred Anderson, author of *George Washington Remembers* addressed the subject of the tribal name given to Washington and its origins:

> George Washington is believed to have been heir to the Seneca title of Caunotaucarius, or Conotocarious, meaning "Destroyer of Villages," "Town Devourer" or "Town Taker," a name which was reportedly first given to his great-grandfather, John Washington (1632–1677) by the Susquehannocks, an Iroquoian people.

Washington, fulfilling his prophetic name, during the American Revolution prosecuted a campaign of genocide to break the power of the *Iroquois*. There had been conflicts and violence upon the frontier and all native people were seen as a threat to settlers. There was never any attempt to sort out and negotiate with those groups who specifically instigated the violence. All native people were held accountable for the acts of a few. Barbara Mann stated:

> To this day, Washington's careful surveying of Ohio in the 1750s and his single-minded dedication to stealing it right up to his death in 1799 are presented with only the vaguest recognition of prior Native proprietary rights, let alone the level of Native suffering that accompanied it's seizure . . . In this text, I rectify some of the omission by walking the reader through the smoldering towns, left in ruins, and the crops, utterly destroyed, year after year, I show the faces of thousands upon thousands of desperate starving refugees fleeing the continental army and its ruthless militias, their children dying on their backs as they ran to yet more misery.

George Washington picked General John Sullivan to lead this campaign during the American Revolution. At the request of the Continental Congress, 4,000 men were assembled with orders from Washington to, ". . . commit utter destruction and devastation and take all the hostages of any age and sex." The force was divided up and Brodhead lead one group up the Allegany River to clear out native people who lived along the riverbanks before he joined up with Sullivan later. Their march began in August of 1779, starting in Easton, Pennsylvania and circled around through the lake country of New York. They implemented the scorched earth policy: indiscriminate burning of every native home, orchard and cornfield they came across, regardless of whether they supported the English or the Americans. Each morning they fired their cannons before their march as a warning they were coming. They did not find any native people to take hostage and met little resistance.

George Washington Anglo-Saxon

I find George Washington to be an excellent example of the ancient Anglo-Saxon cultural values. A farmer and slave owner who dedicated a major part of his life to warrior adventures aimed at controlling larger pieces of land, first for his King and then as an American, for his country. He held large tracts of land and was one of America's largest real estate speculators in the early days. General Washington's family had a major stake in the Ohio Company, a venture with its sights trained on the Northwest territories that had been claimed by the *Iroquois* since the Beaver Wars in the late 1600's—though in truth the land was and had been occupied by the *Mingo*, *Shawnee*, and other *Algonquin* peoples. It has been noted that George Washington did not treat his slaves very well. Michael Coard, cited in his paper, *The Black Eye On George Washington's White House*, a written first hand statement by a visitor to Mount Vernon. The visitor, Julian Niemcewicz, a Polish poet wrote about the slaves there:

> We entered some Negroes' huts, for their habitations cannot be called houses. They are far more miserable than the poorest cottages of our peasants. The husband and wife sleep on a miserable bed, the children on the floor. A very poor chimney, a little kitchen furniture stands amid this misery—a teakettle and cups. They receive a cotton jacket and a pair of breeches yearly.

The National Park Service has been excavating the location of the first White House in Philadelphia. Coard among others have been struggling to get the slaves who lived there with George Washington recognized. At the time Washington occupied the Philadelphia White House, the law in Pennsylvania freed any slave who lived there more than six months. Among other things Mr. Coard told the story of Washington taking his slaves over the border into other states each six months to keep them enslaved. To quote Coard's paper again:

> Washington's treatment, or more precisely his mistreatment, of his fellow men and women went beyond mere stinginess in barely providing food, clothing, and shelter. It applied as well to his disdain for the human worth of his enslaved black laborers as evidenced by his reference to them as "a Species of Property" very much as he described animals like his dogs and horses. As another Washington authority noted, "Most of the slaves who worked his [i.e. Washington's] farms he treated as cattle and referred to only by their first names."

At the conclusion of the American Revolution our new federal government declared those of the *Iroquois* who were still within our boundaries to be conquered peoples, even if they had been our *allies*. The Treaty of Paris affirmed the independence of America envisaged by the Founding Fathers. The treaty also included a clause ordering forfeiture of *Oneida* and *Tuscarawa* territory to the new American rulers. Tribal property boundary lines were repeatedly drawn and redrawn on paper, treaties written and rewritten to change the shrinking territorial boundaries of the native people. The federal attitude toward native groups was akin to an all-powerful parent dictating terms to young children.

This was certainly the accepted mode of operation to be used by Lewis and Clark in 1804 when they were set off on their long journey by Thomas Jefferson. The historian Stephen Ambrose related the condescending manner in which Captain Merriwether Lewis addressed the *Oto*, the first tribe these explorers encountered:

> "Children," he continued, as Clark recorded his speech, "we have been sent by the great Chief of the seventeen great nations to inform you . . . That a great council was lately held between this great chief and your old fathers the French and Spaniards." There it was decided that the Missouri River country now belonged to the United States, so that all those who lived in that great country, whether white or red, "are bound to obey the commands of their great Chief the President who is now your only great father . . . Children," Lewis went on, the president was now "your only father; he is the only friend to whom you can look for protection, or from whom you can ask favors, or receive good councils, and he will take care to serve you, and not deceive you."

Viking eyes admire good iron weapons and hoards of wealth. Cultures that fashion such weapons were, and are, viewed by us as equals. Those that did not, or which didn't hoard and accumulate visible wealth, were seen as childlike peoples, not equals. If they had anything worth taking, we took it. Resistance meant death. The next 100 years of westward expansion, following the relatively nonviolent Lewis and Clark scouting expedition, was a time when resistance by the Indians to these intrusions was countered with increasing violence.

Outward Conquest Beginning With Cuba

In 1890, the American Frontier was officially closed. We controlled the area of this continent that we now take for granted as our country. The country was changing from an agricultural to a manufacturing power. Spain still occupied many of her New World colonies, but the rum and sugar produced on Cuba began to look very close and sweet to American businessmen. In, 1895 the Cubans began an armed resistance against their Spanish occupiers, a rebellion that average Americans could easily identify as similar to their earlier revolution. By this time U.S. businessmen were heavily invested in Cuba, prompting greater federal interest in the outcome. Professor Howard Zinn in his *Peoples History of the United States* quoted President Grover Cleveland who in 1896 said:

> It is reasonably estimated that at least from $30,000,000 to $50,000,000 of American capital are invested in the plantations and in railroad, mining, and other business enterprises on the island. The volume of trade between the United States and Cuba, which in 1889 amounted to about $64,000,000 rose in 1893 to about $103,000,000.

In 1898, the iron long boat, the Maine, steamed into Havana Harbor as a demonstration of our military might. The officers of the ship had orders to remove any endangered American citizens from the city. On the night of February 15th the Maine blew up and sank with 262 sailors aboard. Chalmers Johnson reported in his book, *Sorrows of Empire* that Assistant Secretary of the Navy Theodore Roosevelt declared the incident, "an act of dirty Spanish treachery." A 1976 study by the U.S. Navy suggested that spontaneous combustion in the ship's coalbunker caused the calamity. However at the time of the incident, "Remember the Maine!" became a popular battle cry throughout the land. Roosevelt went on to lecture the Naval College that, "All the great masterful races have been fighting races . . . No triumph of peace is quite so great as the supreme triumph of war."

Slightly more than two months later, on April 25th, Congress officially declared war on Spain. The war in Cuba lasted three months and we lost 325 men. Our American business community also had its eyes on the Philippines, another Spanish colony. We were manufacturing more product than we could sell in the U.S. and American businessmen hungrily looked at China as a market with huge potential. Our merchants needed a secure port in the Orient from which to distribute their products.

The U.S. Asiatic Squadron sailed "The Great White Fleet" into Manila Bay, the Philippines under the command of Commodore George Dewey. By noon the next day his six iron ships had crippled or sunk the entire Spanish fleet anchored there, 9,000 miles from Cuba. Some of the Philippine people were revolting against Spain at that time and with the initial help of the Filipino revolutionaries, America laid the groundwork for occupying another strategically valuable port city half a world away.

The stated objective of the Spanish-American War was Cuban independence, but when the Treaty of Paris was signed on December 10th, 1898 its conclusion served instead to mark two important historical events: the collapse of Spain as a colonial empire; the beginning of American Imperialism. The treaty granted official freedom to Cuba (on our terms), but more realistically it marked the beginning of the United States government's position as a growing global military power with foreign military bases. Many American public and political figures trumpeted a national policy of expansion that was in their view both inevitable and somehow divinely blessed. The treaty also allowed the United States to acquire Puerto

Rico, Guam, and the Philippines for a lump sum of $20,000,000 paid to Spain. Our annexation of the Philippines was interpreted by powerful business interests as the beginning of our U.S. economic expansions in Asia. Naturally, Asians had their own ideas regarding foreign occupation.

Once war on the Cuban front ended our American military following orders from Washington would not formally meet with the local resistance forces who fought alongside us, helping to gain victory against Spain. General William Shafter commanded American forces on the island, and General Calixto Garcia was the Cuban leader. The latter's men were not even permitted to come into town bearing arms. Zinn produced the contents of a letter in his book that General Garcia wrote to General Shafter expressing dismay over the utter lack of dialogue between them:

> I have not been honored with a single word from yourself informing me about the negotiations for peace or the terms of the capitulation by the Spaniards. When the question arises of appointing authorities in Santiago de Cuba . . . I cannot see but with the deepest regret that such authorities are not elected by the Cuban people, but are the same ones selected by the Queen of Spain . . . A rumor too absurd to be believed, general, describes the reason of your measures and of the orders forbidding my army to enter Santiago for fear of massacres and revenge against the Spaniards. Allow me, sir, to protest against even the shadow of such an idea. We are not savages ignoring the rules of civilized warfare. We are a poor, ragged army, as ragged and poor as was the army of your forefathers in their noble war for independence . . .

But the American government had no desire to see a new non-European republic (like Haiti) in the region, and had no intention of allowing the Cubans to manage their homeland. Zinn wrote that "The Cleveland administration said a Cuban victory might lead to 'the establishment of a white and a black republic,' since Cuba had a mixture of two races. And the black republic might be dominant." The historian further reported that the Spanish Minister to the U.S. wrote our Secretary of State to warn that, the results of the Haitian's revolt against France in 1803 would be the same in Cuba: "In this revolution, the negro element had the most important part. Not only the principal leaders are colored men, but at least eight-tenths of their supporters . . . and the result of the war, if the Island can be declared independent, will be a secession of the black element and a black Republic."

Though Cuba was formally handed sovereignty, we kept the control. American businessmen seized the opportunity to act while the U.S. Army took up residence. The United Fruit Company, for example, bought up 1.9 million acres at twenty cents an acre. No real effort occurred to annex the island because of the Teller Amendment, championed by anti-imperialists and passed as Congress declared war, directly forbid annexation.

Instead, in 1901, Senator Orville Platt of Connecticut authored his own amendment to the Army Appropriations Bill that outlined circumstances under which the U.S. government could interfere with Cuban affairs of state and dictate policy. The amendment also stipulated that Cuban representatives would not sign any treaties that might threaten its sovereignty or contract debts that could not be paid with normal revenues. It granted America special privileges to intervene militarily any time it saw fit, and we did so on four occasions between 1906 and 1920. We forced the new Cuban government to make these terms part of its new constitution, along with an article that gave us our first foreign naval base at Guantanamo Bay. This article was written so that the military base must be kept in operation until **both** sides agree it should be removed.

Taking The Philippines

In the Philippines the people did not want to be the property of the United States. In the 1890's a secret Filipino group called the *Katipunan Brotherhood* had formed in the 1776 spirit of the American Freemasons—a secret society through which patriotic minds might meet and form a plan of rebellion against the oppressive Spanish authority. A young man named *Emilio Aguinaldo* joined their ranks in 1895 and grew to heroic stature in the armed conflict that began a year later. The rebels largely operated from broken, mountainous terrain where they could control the fighting.

In 1898, when the Spanish-American War erupted, *Aguinaldo* corresponded with American officials to seek support for his cause. When the U.S. Navy reached the Philippines, Commodore George Dewey warmly welcomed the rebel leader aboard his ship. Commodore Dewey asked for *General Aguinaldo's* aid in defeating the Spanish and assured him that America did not wish to lay a claim on the Filipino homeland.

Historian and novelist William Schroder spoke about the meeting in an interview given to *Rudy Rimando*, President of the Bainbridge Island Filipino American Club on November 29, 2004.

"You've read the American Constitution," he [Dewey] said. "We have no provisions in our law that permit us to take colonies." When Aguinaldo asked

Dewey for written assurance of Filipino independence, Dewey told him to "trust in the goodwill of the American people."

Schroder recounted how the American and Filipino commanders drew up a plan to contain the Spanish in Manila, while at the same time Dewey worked with American army commander Wesley Merritt to secretly negotiate with the Spanish. After the Spanish naval fleet was destroyed, Dewey cut a deal with the defeated enemy to achieve Spanish surrender in exchange for their safe passage out of the harbor. *Aguinaldo's* men dug fourteen miles of trenches around the city to block the Spanish escape by land. While waiting on Dewey's signal to attack, the Filipino revolutionaries gathered and wrote their own constitution for a new government. They were unaware that Dewey had formed a secret agreement with the Spanish. American ships would fire some harmless rounds, then accept the surrender of the Spaniards while guaranteeing that Spanish prisoners would not be turned over to the revolutionaries. It happened just like that. A few token shots were exchanged and U.S. flags were swiftly run up flagpoles all over the city.

The American commander promptly ordered *Emilio Aguinaldo* to disband his army and leave the area, calling the new flag of the Philippine Republic an "unauthorized bunting." When the former revolutionary allies wouldn't leave the American ships opened up their big guns and killed thousands. *Aguinaldo's* men fled into the countryside along with their new president of the Philippine Republic leaving three thousand freedom fighters dead in the trenches. They were stunned and confused by the American actions.

The Americans became the new occupiers to bring

"democracy" to the islands. The enraged Filipinos repeatedly attacked and the Americans struck back. Our superior weaponry was overpowering and we killed between 250,000 and 1,000,000 military and civilian Filipinos during the two-year conflict. *Aguinaldo* was captured in 1901 by General Fredrick Funston, who tricked his way into the Filipino patriot's camp by pretending to be part of a group of captives. All in the party were either armed Americans or hired nationals.

Mark Twain argued that occupying such places betrayed the ideals of democracy itself, the very "gift" our government told the public we were giving the Filipinos. It was also a futile effort that exacted a toll of 4,324 American lives. Twain a famous writer of the time titled an essay on this subject, *To the Person Sitting in Darkness.* The following is an excerpt:

> Our case is simple. On the 1st of May, Dewey destroyed the Spanish fleet. This left the Archipelago in the hands of its proper and rightful owners, the Filipino nation. Their army numbered 30,000 men, and they were competent to whip or starve out the little Spanish garrison; then the people could have set up a government of their own devising. Our traditions required that Dewey should now set up his warning sign, and go away. But the Master of the Game happened to think of another plan—the European plan. He acted upon it. This was, to send out an army—ostensibly to help the native patriots put the finishing touch upon their long and plucky struggle for independence, but really to take their land away from them and keep it. That is, in the interest of Progress and Civilization. The plan developed, stage by stage, and quite satisfactorily. We entered into a military alliance with the trusting Filipinos, and they hemmed in Manila on the land side, and by their valuable help the place,

with its garrison of 8,000 or 10,000 Spaniards, was captured—a thing which we could not have accomplished unaided at the time. We got their help—by ingenuity. We knew they were fighting for their independence, and that they had been at it for two years. We knew they supposed that we also were fighting in their worthy cause—just as we had helped the Cubans fight for Cuban independence—and we allowed them to go on thinking so. Until Manila was ours and we could get along without them. Then we showed our hand. Of course, they were surprised—that was natural; surprised and disappointed; disappointed and grieved. To them it looked un-American; uncharacteristic; foreign to our established traditions. And this was natural, too; for we were only playing the American Game in public—in private it was European. It was neatly done, very neatly, and it bewildered them. They could not understand it, for we had been so friendly—so affectionate, even—with those simple-minded patriots! We, our own selves, had brought back out of exile their leader, their hero, their hope, their Washington-Aguinaldo; brought him in a warship, in high honor, under the sacred shelter and hospitality of the flag; brought him back and restored him to his people, and got their moving and eloquent gratitude for it. Yes, we had been so friendly to them, and had heartened them up so many ways! We had lent them guns and ammunition; advised with them; exchanged pleasant courtesies with them; placed our sick and wounded in their kindly care; entrusted our Spanish prisoners to their humane and honest hands; fought shoulder to shoulder with them against "the common enemy" (our own phrase); praised their courage, praised their gallantry, praised their mercifulness, praised their fine and honorable conduct; borrowed their trenches, borrowed strong positions which they had previously captured from the Spaniards; petted them, lied to them—officially proclaiming that

our land and naval forces came to give them their freedom and displace the bad Spanish Government—fooled
them, used them until we needed them no longer; then
derided the sucked orange and threw it away. We kept
the positions which we had beguiled them of; by and by,
we moved a force forward and overlapped patriot
ground—a clever thought, for we needed trouble, and
this would produce it. A Filipino soldier, crossing the
ground, where no one had a right to forbid him, was shot
by our sentry. The badgered patriots resented this with
arms, without waiting to know whether Aguinaldo, who
was absent, would approve it or not. Aguinaldo did not
approve; but that availed nothing. What we wanted, in
the interest of Progress and Civilization, was the Archi-
pelago, unencumbered by the patriots struggling for independence; and War was what we needed. We clinched
our opportunity. (Printed in the North American Review
in February, 1901.)

In regard to the single murdered Filipino that set off the
fighting, President McKinley told the press that insurgents
started it by, ". . . attacking Manila." He called *Emilio
Aguinaldo* an, ". . . outlaw bandit." Congressional opinion fortified by such justification, was summed up by Senators including Senator Albert Beveridge of Indiana (from a speech on
January 9,1900):

It is America's duty to bring Christianity and civilization to savage and senile peoples. The Philippines are
ours forever . . . We will not renounce our part in the
mission of our race, trustee, under God, of the civilization of the world . . . The Pacific is our ocean . . . My
own belief is that there are not 100 men among them
who comprehend what Anglo-Saxon self-government
even means, and there are 5,000,000 people to be governed. It has been charged that our conduct of the war

has been cruel. Senators, it has been the reverse. Senators must remember that we are not dealing with Americans or Europeans. We are dealing with Orientals.

Such public ethnocentric assertions, so astounding today, became commonplace both before and after the Spanish-American hostilities. Senator Tillman of South Carolina said, "It is absurd to talk about teaching self-government to people racially unfit to govern themselves." President McKinley reportedly told a group of clergymen that he never wanted the islands in the first place. However, that after many sleepless nights spent in prayer an answer came to him from God that the folk of the Philippines were "unfit for self-government." McKinley said that there was, "nothing left for us to do but to take them all and educate the Filipinos, and uplift and civilize and Christianize them, and by God's grace do the very best we could by them, as our fellow men for whom Christ also died."

Whatever our government's pretext, any native resistance stood very little long-term chance against American arms. But, as Zinn pointed out, "The Filipinos did not get the same message from God." The official fighting dragged out over three years, with the insurgency both suffering and inflicting the heavy casualties previously mentioned.

War Resistance

The Anti-Imperialist League formed in 1898 by a group of American citizens protested our actions in the Philippines. This organization circulated letters sent home by soldiers witnessing, and perpetrating atrocities overseas. One reported that the men of the 20th of Kansas swept through the town of Caloocan burning it and killing everyone they could find until there was not one living person left. Many likened killing natives to hunting, and others (some of them black) angrily related the use of "nigger" as a description of the Filipino natives by white soldiers.

Newspapermen in the combat zone described the fighting as an American effort to exterminate the native people. *Soldiers' Letters,* the controversial 1899 pamphlet assembled and published by the Anti-Imperialists, documented the wide range of views by participants in the conflict:

> The boys went for the enemy as if they were chasing jackrabbits . . . I, for one, hope that Uncle Sam will apply the chastening rod, good, hard, and plenty, and lay it on until they come into the reservation and promise to be good "Injuns." (Colonel Funston, Twentieth Kansas Volunteers)

> And bet, I did not cross the ocean for the fun there was in it, so the first one I found, he was in a house, down on his knees fanning a fire, trying to burn the house, and I pulled my old Long Tom to my shoulder and left him to burn with the fire, which he did. I got his knife, and another jumped out of the window and ran, and I brought him to the ground like a jackrabbit. I killed seven that I know of, and one more I am almost sure of: I shot ten shots at him running and knocked him down, and that evening the boys out in front of our trenches now found one with his arm shot off at the shoulder and dead as hell; I had lots of fun that morning. There were five jumped out of the brush and cut one of the Iowa band boys, and we killed every one of them, and I was sent back to quarters in the hurry. Came very near getting a court-martial, but the colonel said he had heard that I had done excellent work and he laughed and said "There's good stuff in that man," and told me not to

leave any more without orders. Well, John, there will always be trouble here with the natives unless they annihilate all of them as fast as they come to them. (Burr Ellis, of Frazier Valley, California)

I deprecate this war, this slaughter of our own boys and of the Filipinos, because it seems to me that we are doing something that is contrary to our principles in the past. Certainly we are doing something that we should have shrunk from not so very long ago. (General Reeve, lately Colonel of the Thirteenth Minnesota Regiment)

General Reeve's assertion that such warring was "contrary to our principles in the past" is true at least in the most generous sense—our nation's stated *principles* hold that we favor self-determination. But in action we have demonstrated far more forcefully that the culture from which our leaders largely descend favors self-determination only for members of the white Anglo-Saxon tribe. General Reeve's point of view was shared by a number of his contemporaries and fellow enlisted men.

Talk about dead Indians! Why, they are lying everywhere. The trenches are full of them . . . More harrowing still: think of the brave men from this country, men who were willing to sacrifice their lives for the freedom of Cuba, dying in battle and from disease, in a war waged for the purpose of conquering people who are fighting as the Cubans fought against Spanish tyranny and misrule. There is not a feature of the whole miserable business that a patriotic American citizen, one who loves to read of the brave deeds of the American colonists in the splendid struggle for American independence, can look upon with complacency, much less with pride. This war is reversing history. It places the American people and the government of the United States in the position occupied by Great Britain in 1776. It is an utterly causeless and defenseless war, and it should be abandoned by this government without delay. The longer it is continued, the greater crime it becomes—a crime against human liberty as well as against Christianity and civilization . . . honest to God, I feel sorry for them. (Theodore Conley, of a Kansas Regiment)

They will never surrender until their whole race is exterminated. They are fighting for a good cause, and the Americans should be the last of all nations to transgress upon such rights. Their independence is dearer to them than life, as ours was in years gone by, and is today. They should have their independence, and would have had it if those who make the laws in America had not been so slow in deciding the Philippine question. Of course, we have to fight now to protect the honor of our country but there is not a man who enlisted to fight these people, and should the United States annex these islands, none but the most bloodthirsty will claim himself a hero. This is not a lack of patriotism, but my honest belief. (Ellis G. Davis, Company A, 20th Kansas)

There was never a formal declaration of war on the Filipinos, and Teddy Roosevelt stated that it was over on July 4, 1902, even though skirmishes continued for fourteen more years. For his role in the affair Dewey was promoted to the special rank, Admiral of the Navy. Most Americans know little about this nasty little war, initiated by us because the Filipinos wanted independence rather than another government controlled by foreigners.

The last resistance came from an Islamic population gathered on the southern islands. United States armed forces maintained martial law and colonial control in the Philippines until after World War II when the Filipinos were granted full independence. There is still violent unrest in some parts of the islands.

Economic interests far outweighed any publicized desire to offer the Filipinos some kind of spiritual awakening or a form of civilization as we defined it. We had an interest in selling our surplus textiles, clothing, shoes and other goods to the new Chinese market. The sheer size of the potential marketplace in China had the American industrialists lusting for Chinese commerce. We needed a secure port close to the point of sale. When push came to shove in this regard, our nation's leaders, with little conscience, rated the Filipino people lower on a sliding scale of humanity. Some citizens termed the whole business as "God's will," and thus completely righteous.

Early 20th Century sociologist pioneer and Yale professor William Graham Sumner is credited with coining the term "**ethnocentrism**," which he defined as:

> . . . the technical name for this view of things in which one's own group is the center of everything, and all others are scaled and rated with reference to it. Folkways correspond to it to cover both the inner and outer relation. Each group nourishes its own pride and vanity, boasts itself superior, exalts its own divinities, and looks with contempt on outsiders. Each group thinks its own folkways are the only right ones, and if it observes [that] the other groups have other folkways these excite scorn.

This judgmental way of viewing other culturally or racially different people is not unique to our culture but it is a very strong viewpoint within our group. Ethnocentrism has often been behind the justification for many of our military actions and the philosophy of dehumanizing people as the enemy. It has come down to us from those Anglo-Saxon peoples who desired the lands of post-Roman Briton. Ethnocentric attitudes of superiority remain with us to this day, a dangerous moral blight, a trap wasting countless lives and causing unimaginable suffering for those caught in its crossfire. The ethnocentric Viking viewpoint we have inherited as a culture keeps us from learning and adopting valuable ideas from ancient cultures we continue to view as simple and childlike. Some of these cultures live in balance with their environment as they have for thousands of years. It is evident that there is nothing new about our foreign military exploits. Let us stop repeating the past.

5

We Sail On To Vietnam

My father landed in Korea during the Christmas season of 1946 after a long voyage aboard one of our long ships, an iron troop transport filled with warriors, sent to enforce a so-called police action. He remembered hearing Koreans say, "*Mee gook, mee gook.*" Many American soldiers found this funny, assuming the Koreans said, "I'm a gook." The Americans had no idea that this was a cordial greeting meaning, "Beautiful country" or "American." The Koreans spoke this short phrase, intending a complimentary greeting to the American soldiers and their faraway homeland.

Growing up in the late 1960s, I heard a lot of talk about "killing gooks," meaning Vietnamese during our undeclared war in Vietnam. My parents and I never felt good about the American war in Vietnam. It made no sense. I was sure if the American people really knew the amount of suffering going on in Vietnam, they would stop the war. After early press coverage on television showed American servicemen lighting huts on fire while crying civilians watched, the American government tightly controlled future press coverage. The images of suffering were not commonly seen on television screens in America. The American people's consent for that war was generally derived from information promoted by government slogans to keep the world free and us safe from Communism. Most Americans knew very little true history of the Vietnamese people. Many years later, I bring to you a clearer picture of the events that led America to the conflict in Vietnam.

Brief History Of Annam Becoming The Colony Of French Indo-China

Vietnam has a long history of resistance, fighting first against the Chinese and later the Europeans. A hundred years before we became involved in the conflict in Southeast Asia, the French had taken control of the area that would become known as Vietnam. In the 1830's, a French Catholic missionary named *Pierre Pigneau de Behaine* provided support to the eventual winners in a civil war. This conflict decided the next Vietnamese royal dynasty. The missionary hoped that this active participation might earn France preferential status with the new leaders. He was mistaken.

When *Gia Long* the new Emperor began his rule at the beginning of the *Nguyen Dynasty* he distrusted the French presence. He did not trust the priests who sought to convert his people from their Buddhist faith to Catholicism. The emperor began a campaign of persecution to drive out the missionaries, executing some who refused to depart. An outcry for retribution rose in Paris, but France did little throughout the 1840s except to demand the release of prisoners.

In 1859, economic and military speculation renewed the

interest of the French in the region. The persecution of missionaries was used as the pretext by Napoleon III to dispatch a naval force there. The French with the help of the Spanish began an invasion of what is today known as Vietnam. The better-armed European invaders conquered the provinces in the Mekong Delta of Cochin China (later called South Vietnam) after a few years of armed struggle. By the 1880s, the Hanoi region (later called North Vietnam) was finally subdued. Vietnam thus became French Indochina, formally titled a protectorate by France. The Vietnamese were forced to support a class of French civil servants who administered law and French business interests. The people of Vietnam lost resources and wealth transferred to France. The French colonists were met with resistance. The next 50 years and extending even beyond that were marked by the bitterness of the occupied for the occupier, a long slow simmer that would rise to a boil shortly before World War II.

The Rise Of Vietnamese Resistance To Colonial Occupation

In the 1920s some Vietnamese traveled to France to work and study. While there they met a different type of Frenchman: the socialist and the communist, and France had their fair share of both. The oppressed Vietnamese workers could relate to the values expressed by these French political groups. Among those who sailed west on merchant ships was a man remembered by history as *Ho Chi Minh*. He served as a cook aboard a steamer before working in London and Paris. He wrote a paper in 1924 called *Condition of the Peasants in Vietnam*. An excerpt described his observation:

The Annamese [Vietnamese] in general are crushed by the blessings of French protection. The Annamese peasants especially are still more odiously crushed by this protection; as Annamese they are oppressed, as peasants they are robbed, plundered, expropriated, and ruined. It is they who do all the labor, all the corvees. It is they who produce for the whole horde of parasites, loungers, civilizers and others. And it is they who live in poverty while their executioners live in plenty, and die of starvation when their crops fail. This is due to the fact that they are robbed on all sides and in all ways by the Administration, by modern feudalism, and by the Church. In former times, under the Annamese regime, lands were classified into several categories according to their capacity for production. Taxes were based upon this classification. Under the present Colonial regime, all this has changed. When money is wanted, the French Administration simply has the categories modified. With a stroke of their magic pen, they have transformed poor land into fertile land, and the Annamese peasant is obliged to pay more in taxes on his fields than they can yield to him . . . One can see that behind the mask of democracy, French imperialism has transplanted in Annam the whole cursed medieval regime, including the salt tax; and that the Annamese peasant is crucified on the bayonet of capitalist civilization and the cross of prostituted Christianity.

Many years before, Thomas Jefferson, Patrick Henry and John Adams motivated by a similar spirit took up their pens against the King of England.

Born in 1890 as *Nguyen Tat Thanh* in a central section of Vietnam, *Ho Chi Minh's* life and career were shaped by the oppression he witnessed during his young life. His father resigned his job as a town official to protest against French domination.

Later, while living in France, *Ho Chi Minh* met and became involved with the French Communist Party. He studied the writings of Lenin and in 1930 he headed the Indochinese Communist Party under his first pseudonym, *Nguyen Ai Quoc* (*Nguyen* the Patriot.) Leaving Europe *Ho Chi Minh* traveled to Hong Kong and then back to Vietnam where he lived in the mountainous frontier near the border of China. He traveled, organized, fomented revolution and actually hid in China from the French. While in China he was arrested and imprisoned by the Chinese as a French spy. In Chinese prison he was starved to the point that his teeth began to fall out. This was before the communist revolution in China.

Ho Chi Minh helped form the League for the Independence of Vietnam in the late 1930s. This organization became known as the *Vietminh*. The *Vietminh* took up arms against their French "protectors." By 1940, the *Vietminh* resistance to French occupation was well underway; 6,000 casualties told the tale of their investment and many thousand more imprisoned.

Massachusetts Institute of Technology professor Harold Issacs traveled to Vietnam to view the political climate before 1947. Issacs wrote in his eyewitness report:

> The hatred of the Annamites for the French was a living, leaping thing in the land. You read it in the faces of the ordinary people, in the faces I saw in the yard of the Saigon Surete. You heard it in the voices of the educated Annamites, speaking impeccable French . . . It was like a social disease of the subjected, this passionate loathing. Whole generations had been infected with it, by the vermin in French prisons or by the slower poison of an enforced inferiority haunting every step of their lives from cradle to grave.

This was hatred compounded of many things. The dull and weary sense of unrepaid toil was part of it; so was the chronic injustice never articulately understood. There was also the nettle of racialism in it, for the masters were white and the least of them was greater than the greatest of the land's own sons. Racialism, where it does not impose dumb submission, outrages manhood and breeds violence.

"Vietminh" is the popular contraction of Viet Nam Doc Lap Dong Minh, the League for Independence of Vietnam. Vietnam, meaning the Land of the South, is the ancient name of the ancient country. The Vietminh was first formed in 1939 as a coalition of various groups: democrats, Socialists, Communists, and other less well defined sections of the independence movement. They agreed primarily on a program of common struggle for independence and a social program based on the idea of a democratic republic.

Ho Chi Minh remained dedicated to inclusive democracy and equality including the recognition of women and the various ethnic minorities living in the region. Even his political enemies admired the personal integrity and resolution of *Ho Chi Minh*, whose last and best-known pseudonym meant The Enlightener. Indeed, the main tenets of *Ho Chi Minh's* platform focused on national freedom, independence, and reform rather than a specifically Communist ideology.

Ho Chi Minh Worked With The United States To Fight The Japanese

Japanese forces began to invade Indochina in 1940, taking it a piece at a time. Lacking the resources to drive them out the French were themselves reduced to a mere figurehead status.

In March of 1945 the Japanese military took control of Indochina and imprisoned the French military. The Japanese took so much from the Indochinese that many starved. The *Vietminh* turned their fight against the Japanese. Americans began working with the *Vietminh* at this point during the war. Supplies were routed through China to units led by *Ho Chi Minh*. Harold Isaacs, author of *No Peace For Asia*, commented on this relationship:

> In March he [Ho Chi Minh] crossed over and was the leader of the bands which made contact with the Americans, received arms and training and liberated large areas in the northern provinces. A small quantity of tommy guns, automatics, radios and other supplies was parachuted to the partisan bands and was soon followed by teams of American officers who entered Indochinese territory and joined the partisan bands in operation against the Japanese.

Beginning in the north, the *Vietminh* with American support fought their way southward. By early August 1945 when they reached Hanoi, the larger war in the Pacific was over. The *Vietminh* held a congress and formed a provisional government electing *Ho Chi Minh* President. They named their country, The Democratic Republic of Vietnam. The *Emperor Bao Dai* who had held power for the French and then the Japanese, abdicated his throne. In 1945, the *Vietminh* believed they had been befriended by the freedom-loving Americans and entertained what they hoped was a realistic vision for independence and international acceptance. Their governmental representatives moved into offices in Hanoi and Saigon, in the wake of Japan's surrender to the Allied Nations.

The Allied leaders had met earlier at Potsdam and made a

plan for Indochina. Everything was about to change. The Allied leaders plan divided Indochina in half at the 17th parallel, allowing for a cooperative action to drive out the Japanese. China our ally would drive them out of the area north of that line and England was to *restore order* in the south. This is the *first separation* of North and South, Indochina (Vietnam). The *Vietminh* were still mainly in the north, the wealth and fertile farmland was mainly in the south.

The Vietnamese Declaration Of Independence

Soon the British arrived to look things over. *Ho Chi Minh* led 100,000 citizens in a parade and rally in Saigon to show solidarity and offer a proper welcome to the Allied Forces. On September 2nd the provisional government of the new Democratic Republic of Vietnam revealed a Declaration of Independence for Vietnam, based on the works of Jefferson and the French text "Rights of Man and the Citizen." It reads, in part:

> "All men are created equal. They are endowed by their Creator with certain inalienable rights, among these are Life, Liberty, and the pursuit of Happiness."
>
> This immortal statement was made in the Declaration of Independence of the United States of America in 1776. In the broader sense, this means: All peoples on the earth are equal from birth, all peoples have a right to live, to be happy, and free.
>
> The Declaration of the French Revolution made in 1791 on the Rights of Man and the Citizen also states: "All men are born free and with equal rights, and must always remain free and have equal rights." Those are undeniable truths.

Nevertheless, for more than eighty years, the French imperialists, abusing the standard of Liberty, Equality, and Fraternity, have violated our Fatherlands and oppressed our fellow-citizens. They have acted contrary to the ideals of humanity and justice. In the field of politics, they have deprived our people of every democratic liberty.

They have enforced inhuman laws; they have set up three distinct political regimes in the North, the Center and the South of Vietnam in order to wreck our national unity and prevent our people from being united.

They have built more prisons than schools. They have mercilessly slain our patriots; they have drowned our uprisings in rivers of blood. They have fettered public opinion; they have practiced obscurantism against our people. To weaken our race they have forced us to use opium and alcohol . . .

In the autumn of 1940, when Japanese fascists violated Indochina's territory to establish new bases in the fight against the Allies, the French imperialists went down on their bended knees and handed the country over to them.

Thus, from that date, our people were subjected to the double yoke of the French and the Japanese. Their sufferings and miseries increased. The result was that from the end of last year to the beginning of this year, from Quand Tri province to the North of Vietnam, more than two million of our fellow citizens died from starvation . . .

After the Japanese had surrendered to the allies, our whole people rose to regain our national sovereignty and to found the Democratic Republic of Vietnam . . .

For these reasons, we, members of the Provisional Government, representing the whole Vietnamese people, declare that from now on we break off all relations of a colonial character with France . . .

We are convinced that the Allied nations which at Tehran and San Francisco have acknowledged the principles of self-determination and equality of nations, will not refuse to acknowledge the independence of Vietnam. A people who have courageously opposed French domination for more than eighty years, a people who have fought side by side with the Allies against the Fascists during these last years, such a people must be free and independent.

For these reasons, we, members of the Provisional Government of the Democratic Republic of Vietnam, solemnly declare to the world that Vietnam has the right to be a free and independent country—and in fact is so already. The entire Vietnamese people are determined to mobilize all the physical and mental strength, to sacrifice their lives and property in order to safeguard their independence and liberty.

The British military would have none of it. They refused to meet with the leaders of the new government, declaring the Democratic Republic of Vietnam to be a by-product of Japan's occupation and stated that England would communicate with it only through the Japanese army, *which they left armed* to help dominate the Vietnamese. The British declared martial law and had Japanese soldiers help drive out the *Vietminh*. They also re-armed the 5,000 French troops in Japanese prison camps and ordered the disarmament of *Vietminh* militia and police forces. By September 12th British Indian soldiers had arrived to help restore the old social order and evict the new democratic government from their southern capital in *Saigon*, fully setting in motion a restoration of the French occupation. France not only refused to recognize Vietnam's declaration as an independent republic, but when the Vietnamese leadership tried to broker a peaceful resolution France stalled. It led to an eight-year armed conflict between France and the Vietnamese revolutionaries.

Only pre-Communist China recognized Vietnam's legitimacy, even as it raided and looted undefended Vietnamese territory in the north, while pushing out the Japanese. In South Vietnam, a French commando unit under Colonel Cedile attacked the seat of the *Vietminh* government at the Hotel de Ville on September 23rd. Occupants were killed or imprisoned and houses individually searched for other revolutionaries in hiding. By October 12th a coalition of British, French and Japanese troops worked together to secure *Saigon's* perimeter and purge it of *Vietminh*. By December 50,000 French troops were on hand and had wrested control of South Vietnam, in an attempt to get their colony back. They underestimated the Vietnamese resolve to remain free.

The leadership of the Democratic Republic of Vietnam was shocked by the abandonment of the Allied powers, especially the United States. *Ho Chi Minh* made numerous overtures, but Harry Truman failed to give the courtesy of a single reply.

Author Isaacs commented on the situation:

> Annamite nationalists spoke of the United States as men speak of a hope they know is forlorn but to which they desperately cling all the same. Could all the fine phrases of the Atlantic Charter, of the United Nations pact, of President Roosevelt and his successor, really mean nothing at all?
> . . . It seemed [to be so]. For the only indication the Annamites had of America's role in their struggle came in the form of lend-lease weapons and equipment being used against them by the French and British, and the stunning announcement of an American deal with France for the purchase of $160,000,000 worth of vehicles and miscellaneous industrial equipment for the French in In-

dochina . . . "We apparently stand quite alone," said Ho Chi Minh simply.

The U.S. Army no longer used *Ho Chi Minh* as a resistance leader for the Office of Strategic Service (later to become the CIA). The Vietnamese leader and his men may have worked with American soldiers against the Japanese, but the world situation had changed. These same American soldiers, comrades in arms with the Vietminh, resented the French and they could not understand why their friends were being abandoned. The French killed an American soldier who had given them the finger.

Ho Chi Minh initially believed the Communist Party in France would support the Vietnamese liberation movement but he was similarly frustrated by their inaction. Though *Ho Chi Minh's* eventual policies were a conglomeration of various nationalist philosophies bound by the desire for an independent Democratic Republic of Vietnam, he was forever branded a Communist because of statements he made as an activist in the 1930's, when he was first beginning to articulate his worldview.

The French Create The Republic Of Vietnam In The South

Admiral D'Argenlieu was the French High Commissioner for Indochina during this time. He led an effort to return *Emperor Bao Dai* to the throne (though *Bao* was busy enjoying himself in some of Europe's finest nightclubs), and with a group of wealthy businessmen formed what they called the "free" *Republic of Vietnam*—all the while maintaining what amounted to a police state throughout the south. This would become the government that we Americans supported, known to us as South Vietnam. It did not arise from any grass root efforts among the Vietnamese people. The French occupiers and their business friends formed the South Vietnamese government. The *Vietminh* continued efforts to resolve the conflict through diplomatic negotiations, but they insisted upon a unified independent Vietnam.

Only 2,000 men claimed to follow *Ho Chi Minh* at the outset of the renewed fighting against French rule. By the end of the eight-year struggle, several hundred thousand had answered the call to take back Vietnam from the French. In May of 1954 the North Vietnamese dealt France a military humiliation at the Battle of *Dien Bien Phu*. The French decided to make a stand in the area and set up a defensive position. The *Vietminh* forces overran the French with human wave tactics and utilized withering firepower from leftover WWII American Howitzers acquired from China. They killed or wounded 5,000 French troops on the battleground the French unwisely chose to defend, and captured the remaining 10,000 French soldiers alive.

France immediately demanded a conference in Geneva, Switzerland. Eisenhower's Secretary of State, the fervid anti-Communist, John Foster Dulles headed a campaign to immediately support France during the timeframe of what would become the humiliating defeat at *Dien Bien Phu*. Dulles wanted to send in American bombers and drop atomic weapons, but first sought to build a compact with Britain. He felt an international coalition, even such a small one, might create a more legitimate appearance for such action and would help sway Eisenhower to sanction the attack. England debated the merits of Dulles' argument and opted not to join his coalition, so the Secretary of State didn't get his war quite as soon as he wanted it.

Delegates from France, England, Vietnam's *Vietminh*,

Laos, Cambodia, China, the United States, and the USSR met in Geneva, Switzerland. The accord created there temporarily divided the peninsula along the 17th parallel once more, with the final understanding that *Ho Chi Minh's* people would maintain control in the north while France controlled the south. Terms were agreed upon which formulated how the French prisoners would be returned from captivity. Representatives of the government of the Republic of Vietnam created by the French were not invited as a legitimate party to these negotiations. The *Vietminh* agreed to the terms developed at Geneva only on the *promise of nationwide free elections* to be held in 1956, and properly supervised by an International Control Commission composed of representatives from Canada, India and Poland. The entire population of Vietnam would be free to vote in this proposed election, and decide whether to choose the government of the Democratic Republic of Vietnam led by *Ho Chi Minh* or the Republic of Vietnam formed by the French in the south. The *United States would not sign* the agreement and had no intention of allowing this to happen. Our Representative, the great communist chaser, John Foster Dulles would not shake the Chinese representative's hand and walked out of the Geneva conference.

In order to comprehend the events that followed, it is important to clearly outline what was occurring at that time.

FIRST, *Ho Chi Minh* along with many Vietnamese nationalists founded their movement for independence after many years of occupation by a European foreign power bent on controlling Vietnam strictly for French capital gain. In seeking to establish Vietnam as a legitimate, independent, democratic nation, the people of Vietnam created a national assembly that wrote a constitution as a basis of their democratic government. The framework depended upon a cabinet, a legislature, and a president. It did include Communists as part of its political system (just as France did and does to this day). Only two to five seats were allotted members of the Communist Party while the Vietnamese Nationalist Party had 50 seats and the Revolutionary Party 20 seats. These parties created a constitution that guaranteed citizens personal liberties and included protection of the rights of the country's ethnic minorities.

SECOND, the French military set up a government that was never a democracy. They wished to restore the old colonial order that profited their country as it had before World War II. To make their government appear legitimate to the world they finally got the old Emperor *Bao Dai* to return on April 18, 1949. The French created an agreement to include "Cochin China" as an independent state in their French Union. This was a Catholic government in a Buddhist country. Their military forces, meanwhile, had been beefed up to 150,000, including many Germans and other mercenaries. Half of France's military budget went directly to Indochina. By May of 1950, United States Secretary of State Dean Acheson announced military aid to the French government and the Pope announced that he was praying for *Bao Dai*. By 1951 France had spent 2 billion dollars and had 19,000 soldiers killed trying to re-conquer Vietnam. Even then it was mainly U.S. tax dollars that supported the effort. The result was nothing short of tragic for all involved.

Our Involvement Began Amid Anti-Communist Hysteria

Our government took an uninformed stereotypical racist view of the Vietnamese liberation movement as an impending satellite of communist expansion. President Truman ignored pleas from *Ho Chi Minh*. The Vietnamese were not taken seriously and deemed people who could not govern themselves. They were labeled and written off simply as communists not revolutionaries seeking independence for their people. Thus blindly labeled, they became part of the manic urge of the time to stamp out Communism. This type of labeling fit in with the feverish witch-hunt for communists pursued in our own country during the 1950s, when so many citizens, lawmakers and free thinkers were pinned with the red badge of communist treason. In the midst of this atmosphere, our leaders preached to Americans about the risk of a projected "domino-effect," in which first one Third World country would fall to Communism, then one after another in turn would fall, resulting in some catastrophic shift in world order that would be a threat to the American people.

The Democratic Republic of Vietnam agreed to terms at Geneva in 1954 because of the promise that internationally monitored national elections would occur within two years after the agreement. Though France, England, Russia and China signed, the United States did not sign, allegedly fearing Communists were going to shift the world balance of power in their favor. Secretary of State John Foster Dulles, who served under Dwight Eisenhower, had a powerful hand in determining foreign policy, as did Vice President Richard Nixon, who sat with him on the National Security Council. Together they sent up the communist alarm.

> Under the conditions of today, the imposition on Southeast Asia of the political system of Communist Russia and its Chinese Communist ally, by whatever means, must be a grave threat to the whole free community. The United States feels that possibility should not be passively accepted but should be met by united action. This

might involve serious risks. But these risks are far less than those that will face us a few years from now if we dare not be resolute today.

—John Foster Dulles, March 29, 1954

Or, as *Richard Nixon* stated on April 17, 1954:

What is to be done about the war in Indochina? For one it is not one of materials and it wasn't four months ago. More men are needed and the question is how to get them. They will not come from France, for France is tired of the war, as we were tired of Korea . . . *But the Vietnamese lack the ability to conduct a war by themselves or to govern themselves.* If the French withdrew, Indochina would become Communist-dominated within a month.

The United States as a leader of the free world cannot afford further retreat in Asia. It is hoped the United States will not have to send troops there, but if this government cannot avoid it, the Administration must face up to the situation and dispatch forces.

Both men were so blinded by their particular ideology that they could not interpret the available facts in a realistic way. History has proved both men's arguments against the *Vietminh* were absolutely wrong; their advice to the American people and to our leadership proved to be bad advice. The forces within the country that we were resisting proved irresistible and we finally had to give up. The country became the independent nation it is today, not a strategic threat to us, although they have taken some of our manufacturing jobs. The country of Vietnam today is a popular tourist destination and a member of the World Trade Organization. They have not become an enemy threatening the American people. The Vietnamese obviously can govern themselves.

In fact, the end results of the arguments of these leaders and other promoters of the war caused terrible suffering. Both men had Eisenhower's trust and they applied considerable pressure upon him, demonstrating how the will of a few well-connected people can lead directly to calamitous policies for a vast number of people, American or otherwise. Dulles, the war hawk served to play upon and inflame the fears of American citizens already frightened by Senator Joseph McCarthy's twisted witch-hunt for American Communists.

Secretary of State John Foster Dulles, a Wall Street lawyer, was grandson to another Secretary of State (John Foster). Allen Dulles, John's brother, headed the CIA under Eisenhower. Their elite family produced important government leaders who influenced our foreign policies. John Dulles was very active in the Presbyterian community and delivered stern sermons from his pulpit, condemning the atheistic Communists. His political and religious pronouncements give us another example of the Christian privileged ruling elite and its support of Viking-style warfare.

Twenty years of American involvement in Vietnam negatively altered the world political climate. The war created a legacy of trauma and brutality. At least 56,000 American soldiers were directly killed doing their duty there. An estimated 2 million citizens of Vietnam caught in the horror of the war were also killed. The United States entered this conflict on the side of the French capitalists, crusading against any ideology bearing the slightest resemblance to Communism. We actually climbed into the middle of a revolutionary war for independence and supported the colonial occupying forces.

The Catholic Ngo Family Rulers In A Buddhist Country

In South Vietnam *Emperor Bao Dai*, as leader of the Republic of Vietnam, actually supported the Geneva agreement regarding the national elections if the United Nations acted as a monitor. His hand picked premier, *Ngo Dinh Diem*, did not share this view, because he understood that a free election would mean the loss of his personal power. He and his constituents (largely businessmen, the Catholic minority, French-influenced army officers) instead favored increasingly repressive measures to retain their power. *Ngo Dinh Diem* was NOT popularly elected, *but handpicked and appointed by* the emperor to handle the matters of state. One of *Diem's* brothers, *Ngo Dinh Thuc* a Catholic priest, was archbishop of Saigon and spent a great deal of time in the United States. Another brother, *Ngo Dinh Nhu*, was named head of the National Police, and profited from the drug trade and prostitution in the manner of a gang lord.

One part of the 1954 Geneva agreement was the provision that 300 days after the signing, every Vietnamese citizen was free to choose which part of the country they wished to live. One million moved south, 650,000 of them Catholics (who had supported the French fight against the *Vietminh*) and many of the rest were former French colonial military families. About a third as many migrated north to join with the *Vietminh*. Because of *Diem's* family connection with the Catholic Church and their association with Cardinal Spellman, the Catholic migration got a lot of press in the U.S. The immigrants who moved to the south were aided by the Catholic International Relief Agency, broadening sympathy in American minds for the government of South Vietnam. Throughout the whole of Vietnam, 90 percent of the population was Buddhist. *Diem* gave the Buddhist majority little attention beyond his contempt.

The Geneva conference had stipulated that neither north nor south could bring in foreign military aid. Instead of cooperating with the provision, Emperor *Bao Dai* and *Diem* ignored it as did the United States.

> We did not sign the Geneva Agreements. We are not bound in any way by these agreements, signed against the will of the Vietnamese people.
>
> —*Ngo Dinh Diem* on July 16, 1955

Diem further thumbed his nose at the accord by bringing in American military personnel to train his Army of the Republic of Vietnam (ARVN). Among his supporters in the United States, Cardinal Spellman publicly belittled the Geneva peace summit that had ended French hostilities with wildly ignorant public statements:

> If Geneva and what was agreed upon there mean anything at all, it means taps for the buried hopes of freedom in Southeast Asia! Taps for the newly betrayed millions of Indochinese who must now learn the awful facts of slavery from their eager Communist masters! Now the devilish techniques of brainwashing, forced confessions, and rigged trials have a new locale for their exercise. Americans must not be lulled into sleep by the indifference nor be beguiled by the prospect of peaceful co-existence between two parties if one of them is continually clawing at the throat of the other . . . Do you peacefully coexist with men who thus would train the youth of their godless, Red world?
>
> —Cardinal Spellman on August 31, 1954

Spellman was a close friend of Joseph Kennedy, and they introduced lobbyists for *Diem's* government to important U.S. legislators and editors at media outlets such as *Time* and *Life* magazines and the *New York Times*. These meetings resulted in articles in those publications supporting the migrant Vietnamese Catholics. These actions helped consolidate and solidify American public sentiment for the government in South Vietnam. Once more we see the power wielded by a few well-connected Americans on public opinion.

In 1955, *Ngo Dinh Diem* seized control of the Republic of Vietnam from the emperor who had put him into power. With *Bao Dai* out of the picture, he instituted manhunts for those who resisted his will and he began calling *Ho Chi Minh's* followers *Vietcong*. The new ruler lived with his family in the manner of landed European aristocracy, occupying a palace and controlling his empire through whatever means he found necessary. The brutality of his regime met with increased resistance from the common people as oppression worsened. Peasants were already furious that he had reclaimed land given to them by the *Vietminh* and gifted it to his wealthiest supporters. *Diem* further enraged the lower classes by continually persecuting practitioners of traditional religions and rounding up anyone suspected of communist sympathies. Ironically, the religious and political background that first made him attractive to the Western world also became his personal downfall.

Eight years after his reign began, the Buddhists under *Diem's* control had had enough. In May, Buddhists in *Hué* formally requested to fly their flag in commemoration of Buddha's 2,587[th] birthday. *Diem's* government flatly refused their petition. National police killed nine demonstrators participating in the huge protest that followed. *Diem* sought to place the blame for these deaths on the *Vietminh*, but international photographers witnessed the event and documented the real killers. U.S. supporters appealed to *Diem* to reason with his opposition, but he would not, believing that his family and form of government represented the true God and that Buddhism was not a serious religion.

The National Liberation Front pledged itself to the reunification of Vietnam. Ongoing protests led to a continuing erosion of *Diem's* power, causing considerable discomfort to American officials who had previously supported him. Buddhists invariably contacted foreign correspondents to alert them of upcoming protests and ensure that there was ample international press coverage. These rallies climaxed on June 11, 1963, when an elderly monk named *Thich Quang Duc* sat down in an intersection, poured gasoline over his head and lit his body on fire as a protest against the government that was oppressing the Buddhists. The *Life* magazine photos of this immolation shocked civilian observers in the United States and around the world. The repressive acts of the regime we were supporting became an embarrassment to the United States.

The South Vietnamese combat police deployed by *Diem's* brother attacked Buddhist temples and captured leaders, while other Buddhist leaders found safe haven in the American Embassy.

By autumn 1963 a group of Army of the Republic of Vietnam (ARVN) generals hatched a plot to overthrow *Ngo Diem*, their civilian leader. Our leadership knew it was coming and may have encouraged it. The CIA and U.S. Ambassador Henry Cabot Lodge were kept abreast by CIA operative Lucien Conein, with whom the plotters shared every step of their planning. The coup happened swiftly. On the first of November ARVN troops attacked the *Ngo's* Palace, while *Diem* made a frantic phone call to the U.S. ambassador H.C. Lodge. Lodge claimed he didn't know what the White House perspective might be, and excused himself from the phone by telling *Diem* he could call back if there was anything the Americans could do for his safety. *Diem* and his brother *Nhu* captured by the ARVN forces were then loaded into a truck and removed from the area. The next day, they were put to death. Our leaders were told it was suicide, but their execution had happened in a Catholic Church. R. Andrew Kiel wrote about General Maxwell Taylor's notes on Presidents Kennedy's reaction to the news in his book *J. Edgar Hoover: The Father of the Cold War:*

> . . . shortly after we had seated ourselves around the cabinet table, a member of the White House staff entered and passed the President a flash message from the situation room. The news was that Diem and Nhu were both dead, and the coup leaders were claiming their deaths to be suicide. Kennedy leaped to his feet and rushed from the room with a look of shock and dismay on his face which I have never seen before. He had always insisted that Diem must never suffer more than exile and had been led to believe or had persuaded himself that a change in government would be carried out without bloodshed . . . The degree of American complicity has often been raised, but here again I know of no evidence of direct American participation in carrying out the coup and certainly in the assassination.

President Kennedy's Resistance
To American Invasion

American-sponsored South Vietnamese Army Generals now ran the country under the watchful control of their financiers in the American government. American involvement in Vietnam was a part of our foreign policy that President Kennedy inherited from President Eisenhower and Vice President Richard Nixon. The planned overthrow of Castro known as the Bay of Pigs was another remnant of this previous policy.

Earlier when John F. Kennedy was elected to the United States Senate he made several trips to different places around the world to see first hand what was going on in areas important to American foreign policy. In the fall of 1951 he went to Vietnam and took his younger brother Robert along. They experienced the country under French colonialism. Kiel described Kennedy's impressions and the repercussions:

> Roger Hilsman, who worked in the State Department under President Kennedy, remembers Kennedy stating, "In Indochina we have allied ourselves to the desperate effort of a French regime to hang onto the remnants of an empire."
>
> Following an interview with French commanding General Jean Marie de Lattre, the General sent a message to the State Department stating that the Kennedys were attempting to undermine French policy. The Kennedys' anti-colonial and French views were seen as harming the war effort.
>
> In 1960, Kennedy observed:
>
> Indochina presents a clear case study in the power of anticolonial revolution sweeping Asia and Africa. What has happened also demonstrates that national independence can lead to genuine resistance to Communism. It is a long, sad story with a hopeful chapter, but the end is not in sight. On a trip to Asia in 1951 I saw firsthand that in Indochina we had allied ourselves with a colonial regime that had no real support from the people.

President Kennedy did not want to see Vietnam become an American fought war. John Kennedy experienced considerable

Cabinet pressure to "save" Vietnam from "the Communists."
As early as 1961, Kennedy's advisors had prodded him toward
open-ended military commitment to Southeast Asia. Kiel
stated:

> McNamara, and advisors U. Alexis Johnson,
> William Bundy, Walt Rostow, Secretary of State Dean
> Rusk, National Security Advisor McGeorge Bundy, as
> well as the Joint Chiefs and the Vice-President, were in
> favor of intervention. Advisors Chester Bowles and
> Roger Hilman were known to be against intervention.
> The final decision was was John Kennedy's and he re-
> fused. The record of the November 15, 1961 National
> Security Council meeting makes Kennedy's point clear.

John Kennedy's position was that American troops should
be used only as a last resort and only be dispatched as part of a
multi-national force sanctioned by the United Nations. President Kennedy, a politician who wanted to win re-election
could not come out and publicly state his views but privately
he spoke to confidantes. Kiel provided this quote:

> Kenny O'Donnel stated that Kennedy told him, "I'll
> be damned everywhere a Communist appeaser, but I
> don't care. Once I'm re-elected, I'll withdraw all troops."
> Arthur Schlesinger recalls Kennedy stating in early
> 1963: They want a force of American troops. They say
> it's necessary in order to restore confidence and maintain
> morale. But it will be just like Berlin. The troops will
> march in; the bands will play; the crowds will cheer; and
> in four days everyone will have forgotten. Then we will
> be told we have to send in more troops. It's like taking a
> drink. The effect wears off, and you have to take another.
> The war in Vietnam [he added] could only be won so
> long as it is *their war*. If it were ever converted into a

white man's war, we would lose as the French had lost a decade earlier.

By the spring of 1963, Kennedy was already very tired of the situation, especially with the Buddhist protests exposing the true colors of the government we were supporting there. President Kennedy set a timetable to have all American soldiers out of Vietnam within two years, which would have been shortly after his projected run for re-election in 1964. The president also ordered that the withdrawal begin that same fall. Instead, Kennedy was shot dead less than three weeks after *Premier Ngo Dinh Diem*. At the time of President Kennedy's death we had 16,000 American soldiers, advising and training soldiers in Vietnam with a total of 78 Americans killed in action.

Lyndon Johnson's Support Of American Invasion

President Kennedy's death put the problem of the Vietnam War in the hands of Vice President Johnson whose actions proved very different from President Kennedy's intended schedule for withdrawal. Within two days after the assassination of Kennedy Lyndon Johnson held a major Cabinet meeting and ordered stronger support for the Generals running South Vietnam.

Successive coups in South Vietnam failed to produce a government the United States could popularly champion. A series of generals assumed control of the army and government financed by the United States. We enforced our support of the un-elected Directorate of Generals, as Lyndon Johnson proved far less hesitant than his predecessor to send American soldiers overseas. During his 1964 bid for re-election Johnson made statements to persuade the nation that he believed "American boys" should not "do the fighting for Asian boys." After winning the election, he immediately sent in the Marines to Vietnam, deploying two additional battalions to land at *Da Nang* on March 8th, 1965. By April 20th there were 8,500. By the end of May 1965 there were 46,500 in the fight on Vietnamese soil. In 1968, there were 500,000 American servicemen occupying the country in the undeclared war.

In April of 1965 Johnson spoke at John Hopkins University and stated:

> Tonight Americans and Asians are dying for a world where each people may choose its own path to change. Vietnam is far from this quiet campus. We have no territory there, nor do we seek any. The war is dirty and brutal and difficult. And some 400 young men, born into an America bursting with opportunity and promise, have ended their lives in Vietnam's steaming soil.
>
> Why must we take this painful road? Why must this nation hazard its ease, its interest, and its power for the sake of a people so far away?
>
> We fight because we must fight if we are to live in a world where every country can shape its own destiny. And only in such a world will our own freedom be finally secure . . .
>
> The world as it is in Asia is not a serene or peaceful place. The first reality is that North Vietnam has attacked the independent nation of South Vietnam. Its object is total conquest. Of course some of the people of South Vietnam are participating in this attack on their own government. But trained men and supplies, orders and arms, flow in a constant stream from the North to the South. This support is the heartbeat of the war.
>
> Why are these realities our concern? Why are we in

South Vietnam? We are there because we have a promise to keep. Since 1954 every American President has offered support to the people of South Vietnam. We have helped to build, and we have helped to defend. Thus, over many years, we have made a national pledge to help South Vietnam defend its independence. And I intend to keep that promise.

We are also there because there are great stakes in the balance. Let no one think for a moment that retreat from Vietnam would bring an end to conflict. The battle would be renewed in one country and then another. The central lesson of our time is that the appetite of aggression is never satisfied. To withdraw from one battlefield only means to prepare for the next. We must say in Southeast Asia, as we did in Europe, in the words of the Bible: "Hitherto shalt thou come, but no farther." There are those who say that all our effort there will be futile, that China's power is such it is bound to dominate all Southeast Asia.

And we do this to convince the leaders of North Vietnam, and all who seek to share their conquest, of a very simple fact:

We will not be defeated.

We will not grow tired.

We will not withdraw, either openly or under the cloak of a meaningless agreement. We know that air attacks alone will not accomplish all these purposes. But it is our best and prayerful judgment that they are a necessary part of the surest road to peace.

And until that bright and necessary day of peace we will try to keep conflict from spreading. We have no desire to devastate that which the people of North Vietnam have built with toil and sacrifice. We will use our power with restraint and with all the wisdom we can command. But we will use it.

We will do all this because our own society is at stake.

—Reprinted in the Department of
State Bulletin, LII

Lyndon Baines Johnson was either lying, greatly misled, or badly uniformed about what was actually happening within Vietnam as a whole. His hypotheses were not correct. I do not know upon what facts or advice he made his judgments, but I have read he took the actions of the *Vietminh* personally. It was a matter of ego with him that the little yellow people could stand up to the American fighting machine. He said it was a war but Congress never declared it as such, neither then nor when Nixon, one of the original salesmen of the war, took over the helm after him.

The arguments that the American pro-war leaders offered the American people in support of our military actions in Vietnam turned out to be untrue. After we pulled out our military forces, advisors, and support for the government that the French had created in South Vietnam, the new unified country of Vietnam became in *no way a threat to the people of the United States of America*. Vietnam is now a growing manufacturing center and tourist destination seeking to be a trading partner with the world. Young American men and women went to war, doing what they were told by their elders, and many believed such service itself was an honorable act for the cause of freedom.

Freedom is a very deep and ancient chord played upon Anglo-Saxon heartstrings. They were originally freemen. As inheritors of that spirit, we were ready to fight if told that someone or a group threatens our freedom or for that matter, others' freedom. We now live in a culture affected by those same sentiments, a warrior culture in which many men and now women seek honor by becoming good warriors defending freedom.

The crucial point is members of our government fostered a sense of hysteria that suggested people of Vietnam they called Communists were going to take something from us. These members of our government actually misled us. Those who led us into these wars and their perceptive speechwriters instinctively knew our cultural traits of honor and fear and played upon them with slogans, not truth. Most Americans then and now understand very little about the country known as Vietnam and its social dynamics over the last 150 years. We only know what we have been told by the media and what we have read in our culturally biased public school textbooks. Much like the old *Aenglish,* we have always been ready and willing to fight and sacrifice in honor for the greater good of the tribe or king. Appealing to the masses through the media, playing upon our historic character strengths, our leaders have repeatedly coerced or misled American men and women into military action all over the world. This was accomplished each time by persuading Americans that they were doing the honorable thing. To this day we lead the world in these types of military actions.

6

Costs Of Our
Cultural Militarism And
Hoarding Of Wealth

I t is Memorial Day 2005. The day we remember those
who sacrificed their lives for our country. I am looking at
the front page of my local newspaper and the image there
depicts the face of a tortured soul looking back at me. His face
is slightly twisted, his spirit wrestling with images of things
that happened over 30 years ago, when as a young man, he
was fighting in Vietnam. The headline reads, "The Wounds of
War." Thirty-four years ago the 19 year-old was assigned a job
as a gunner on a helicopter that transported American soldiers
in and out of the jungles of Vietnam. He speaks of the image
of a young Vietnamese boy with no shirt who was gunned
down as he watched. The boy was obviously not a threat to
anyone. "I couldn't understand why he had to die. He was just
a boy with no shirt or shoes, so he couldn't have had any

weapons." This veteran physically survived his tour of duty but his soul is tormented. This is one of the hidden costs of war that individuals and the greater society live with as a result of our militarism then and now.

When we think of the costs of war, we usually think of dollars and lives lost. The lives lost are tragic but there are other consequences of war. There are the physically wounded, and the psychologically wounded. Lt. Colonel Dave Grossman wrote an insightful book in 1995 titled, *On Killing—The Psychological Cost of Learning to Kill in War and Society*. It is a summary of research on battlefield behaviors related to killing in war and the effects it has upon the men who participate in killing and in battle. Grossman pointed out the research of General S.L.A. Marshall during World War II who found that only 15–20 percent of combat infantry fired to kill the enemy when presented with the opportunity. Most Americans do not believe this statement because it is contrary to combat stories we have seen on TV and in the movies.

Innate Human Resistance To Killing Fellow Human Beings

The soldiers who wouldn't fire were called non-firers. Lt. Grossman backed up this research with several similar studies done in England and Israel that substantiate unwillingness to kill as a normal mode of human behavior. General Marshall found out that men by and large have a strong resistance to killing their fellow men.

The Army used this information and modern psychological methods to develop methods of training that overrode these innate resistance mechanisms in their young recruits. By the time of the Korean War, the Army had developed a 50 percent rate of shooters and by Vietnam they got it up to 90 percent. Lt. Dave Grossman was a psychology professor at the U.S. Military Academy. Lt. Grossman said the methods the Army used (and still uses) are operant conditioning, desensitization, and denial defense mechanisms. Using these psychological methods the Army can overcome the natural inborn resistance to fire and kill, but not the internal reaction to the event that happens later. Our soldiers in Vietnam were the youngest in our history. Their consciences were not fully developed. They were taught in basic training to react quickly and fire at the pop-up targets without thinking. Grossman stated:

> During the Vietnam era millions of American adolescents were conditioned to engage in an act against which they had a powerful resistance. This conditioning is a necessary part of allowing a soldier to succeed and survive in the environment where society has placed him. . . . But if society prepares a soldier to overcome his resistance to killing and places him in an environment in which he will kill, then that society has an obligation to deal forthrightly, intelligently, and morally with the psychological event and its repercussions upon the soldier and the society. Largely through an ignorance of the processes and implications involved, this has not happened with the Vietnam veteran.

At the beginning of this chapter I mentioned the veteran disturbed by his wartime memories, and there are many other combat veterans still suffering from what they saw or what they did to survive. Different groups believe that there are between 500,000 and 1,500,000 American veterans who are mentally tortured by what they saw and or did in Vietnam. That is up to 50 percent of the living veterans. The fact that the man and so many veterans are tortured by their conscience for acts that were committed by young men thrown into bad situations trying to do their duty as they were told is a sad but hopeful sign. It shows me that we human beings by and large have a strong force within ourselves that resists killing our fellow human beings. S.L.A. Marshall stated, "The average and healthy individual has such an inner and unusually unrealized resistance towards killing a fellow man that he will not of his own volition take life if it is possible to turn away from that responsibility. At the vital point the soldier becomes a conscientious objector."

I worked for many years with a psychologist who had been a foot soldier in Vietnam during the war. He told me long ago, that as veterans grew older, their consciences progressively developed including a greater understanding of life so that events that occurred in Vietnam come back and haunt them. This is one form of Post Traumatic Stress Disorder (PTSD). Grossman's work substantiated most healthy human beings do have a strong conscience and they can have PTSD for many reasons even if they don't directly kill people themselves. The act of supporting the killing by being there, and seeing death and mutilation can cause extreme guilt. I don't want to dwell here to deeply on this subject, but it is important understand the struggles humans face within themselves after exposure to combat. The support or lack of support a veteran receives from peers and the larger society when the veteran returns home is another contributing factor that may cause turmoil for individual veterans.

In wars before Vietnam, (for example, my father's experience in Korea), Army units were shipped off together on a long boat ride in the great iron ships to where the battle was raging on land. The unit fought together and the survivors returned home together on another long boat ride. The soldiers had time together to talk about their experiences among themselves and support each other. When they arrived home, they were received like heroes by a nation that supported their sacrifice. By contrast the Vietnam foot soldier flew to Vietnam alone, was quickly put in a unit that had lost men, and then when his individual time was up he was flown back without his unit to the U. S. After a few days he was back home on the street where the nation was very divided about support for the war and his sacrifice was not rewarded by a hero's welcome home. A society's reaction to a returning veteran of war and peer support can be ingredients in the formula that affect the development of Post Traumatic Stress Disorder.

Because our nation is involved in continual international conflict, I recommend all concerned citizens read David Grossman's book, as it will change forever how you view the humanity of a combat soldier.

Grossman wrote:

> We may never understand the nature of this force in man that causes him to strongly resist killing his fellow man, but we can give praise for it to whatever force we hold responsible for our existence.
>
> The resistance to the close-range killing of one's own species is so great that it is often sufficient to overcome the cumulative influences of the instinct for self-protection, the coercive forces of leadership, the expectancy of peers, and the obligation to preserve the lives of comrades.
>
> The soldier in combat is trapped within this tragic Catch-22. If he overcomes his resistance to killing and kills an enemy soldier in close combat, he will be forever burdened with the blood guilt, and if he elects not to kill, then the blood guilt of his fallen comrades and the shame

of his profession, nation, and cause lie upon him. He is damned if he does, and damned if he doesn't.

There are many direct costs and many indirect hidden costs to our cultural/national militarism and the hoarding of wealth that it supports. I would like us to openly examine these costs and then re-evaluate the wisdom and appropriateness of the actions.

Huge Military Spending Priority

Today in 2007, American working people pay the largest share of our costly national military budget, both now and in the past. I venture to say that the total real costs are greater than any one of us can imagine. These costs are on many levels aside from dollars and cents expenditures. Many of the dollar costs the American working families pay out through taxes are for the profits of the corporate contractors and international lenders. The full monetary cost is largely hidden from our view. There is almost no way for the average citizen to find out where their tax dollars are actually spent. Even at a United States governmental document repository like the one at Western Michigan University Library all you will find are general statements about expenditures with very little specifics. Government spending is BIG business. There is also a great debt that we are incurring with our lavish contractual indulgences, a debt greater than we can comprehend because the numbers are so huge.

We Americans currently spend over **half** of our discretionary budget on our military. In 2007 the discretionary budget of the United States of America was around 870 billion dollars. The President and Congress decide how to spend these tax revenues each year during the creation of the annual budget bill. The bulk of the remaining federal expenditures are entitlements that are paid through laws that qualify the recipients for benefits such a Social Security, retirements, Medicare, and Medicaid. *Budgets are expressions of a group of people's priorities.*

The military spending portion of our national budget has increased steadily since the beginning of our nation. The first time it was greatly expanded came during the Civil War years. The military budget grew very large during World War II. In the years directly before World War II, we had 186,000 men in the military and today we have over 1,400,000 members of the military. During World War II, a huge bureaucracy and a huge military industrial complex developed to provide the necessary supplies and manpower required by the military for that war effort. After the war, the huge military industrial complex never went away. It is a fact that governmental bureaucracies are born much easier than they die. Once created these huge recipients of American tax dollars begin to protect themselves and their own self-interest with a natural tendency to grow.

Over 725 American Foreign Military Bases

Former CIA consultant and military officer, Professor Chalmers Johnson, author of *The Sorrows of Empire* outlined the growth of this military industrial complex. He points out that today, America has over 725 military bases in at least 38 different countries outside the United States, bases that we maintain every day along with 969 separate bases in our own country. He wrote in the beginning of his book:

> As distinct from other peoples on this earth, most Americans do not recognize—or do not want to recognize—

that the United States dominates the world through its military power. Due to government secrecy, they are often ignorant of the fact that their government garrisons the globe. They do not realize that a vast network of American military bases on every continent except Antarctica actually constitutes a new form of empire.

We are the only country today with military bases all over the world. He said the underlying message is, "The United States prefers to deal with other nations through the use or threat of force rather than negotiations, commerce, or cultural interaction and through military-to-military, not civilian-to-civilian, relations." The dollars and cents cost of this military build-up takes money from the American working people that could be used for education, infrastructure, and health care. These services suffer from either a lack of funding or availability for the general American population. However, because our budget is created largely in secrecy and only disclosed to the average person in very general statements, we only have access to bits and pieces of budgetary information rather than the complete figures. These days we are closing domestic military bases while building more such bases around the globe, especially around the new oil frontier at or near the Caspian Sea.

Chalmers Johnson wrote about such imperialism:

> The simplest definition of imperialism is the domination and exploitation of weaker states by stronger ones. The characteristic institution of so-called neocolonialism is the multinational corporation covertly supported by an imperialist power. The multinational corporation partly replicates one of the earliest institutions of imperialism, the chartered company. In classically mercantilist organizations, the imperialist country authorized a private

company to exploit and sometimes govern a foreign territory on a monopoly basis and then split the profits between government officials and private investors. The best known of these were the English East India Company, formed in 1600; the Dutch East India Company, created in 1602; the French East India Company in 1664; and the Hudson's Bay Company in 1670. The chartered company and the modern multinational corporation differ primarily in that the former never pretended to believe in free trade whereas the multinational corporations use "free trade" as their mantra.

America's foreign military enclaves, though structurally, legally, and conceptually different from colonies, are themselves something like micro-colonies in that they are completely beyond the jurisdiction of the occupied nation. The United States virtually always negotiates a "status of forces agreement" (SOFA) with the ostensibly independent "host" nation. At the time of the terrorist attacks on New York and Washington in September 2001, the United States had publicly acknowledged SOFAs with ninety-three countries, though some SOFAs are so embarrassing to the host nation that they are kept secret, particularly in the Islamic world.

The American people or their representatives in Washington D.C. seem to value the military much more than any other services provided through our national budget. In the fiscal year 2007 over half the discretionary budget is dedicated to the military at near 440 billion dollars with another 33 billion dollars for Homeland Security. The next largest area of expenditure would be Health and Human Services coming in at 68 billion dollars and then Education at 54 billion dollars. You can see that the American people or the government that is supposed to represent us really values the military more than education or health care. Looking at our budget historically when Carter left office in 1979 our military budget was around 179 billion. It has grown to become a huge millstone around the neck of the American taxpayer since the funds needed to support this massive military budget are taken from our paychecks each week. It causes all other areas of public spending to operate in an atmosphere of scarcity.

National Debt Over 9 Trillion

The growth of the military budget has caused the growth of the national debt. The national debt as of December 30, 2007 was $9,128,028,404,782.78. That is over 9 trillion dollars. The debt is currently growing at a rate of 1.36 billion dollars a day. This debt is owed various lenders by the taxpayers of the United States. The CIA website says there are 151 million workers including the unemployed in the United States. Each worker owes around $60,450.50 to somebody. If each worker paid equally on this debt, we would each pay $3,022.53 annually at the rate of 5 percent, which is the approximate current rate of interest. To me as a working person that is a lot of money and I don't appreciate having to pay it. The negative aspect to this debt is that we have never begun to pay on the actual principal of the debt. Supposedly, during the Clinton administration the growth of the actual debt had stopped. This debt is a millstone around the neck of the working people and we will pass it on to our children and grandchildren. This is very unfair since a future generation did not create the debt but they will have to pay for it.

The War Resisters League believes that 80% of the national debt is from the military and if we add the annual interest on the debt and another 70 billion dollars each year for veteran benefits, we will see a much larger chunk of our national yearly tax revenues going to the military. Chalmers Johnson's hypothesis is that *this spending pattern is going to drive our country into bankruptcy*.

Ten years ago in a graduate level budget class, I learned that corporations are paying less tax while individuals are paying more of the total federal tax burden. I also learned that one measure of the equity of taxes is whether those who pay the tax get their fair share of services from that tax. These military bases that have been built around the world generally exist to protect corporate investment, not to protect my lifestyle as a working person. As an American working person, my wages shrink when American corporations use the world labor force.

The American federal government was originally designed to be openly accountable for review of its spending and the process was intended to be open for examination by the people it represented. Article One of The Constitution of the United States of America contains this statement: "No money shall be drawn from the Treasury, but in Consequence of Appropriations made by Law; and a regular Statement and Account of the Receipts and Expenditures of *all* public Money shall be published from time to time." So much of our tax money today is spent in secrecy. What happened to accountability?

Let's briefly compare the amount of money our country of 300 million people spends on the military each year with England and Canada and let's see how our level of spending compares with theirs. England has a population of 60.5 million people. They currently spend roughly 41.3 billion dollars on the military each year. If we divide their population into ours we get a factor of 4.9. Multiply that times the 41.3 billion dollars and you get 202 billion dollars. Our country spends over twice as much per person on the military as England and they are a fairly militarist country. Canada our neighbor to the north has 32.8 million people, divide that into our population and you get a factor of around 9. They spend roughly 9.1 billion dollars on their military. Multiply that times 9 for an equivalency and you get 81.9 billion dollars per year. We spend at least five times more per person on the military than Canada. Canada can afford to provide all their citizens with health care. The next two largest countries spend much smaller amounts of money on their military. Russia spends around 65.2 billion dollars per year and China spends 56 billion dollars. This is one comparative measure of the cost to maintain a military industrial complex of such size and international presence.

Our military spending is way out of line if you use the spending per citizen of other countries as a measure of evaluation. The working people of our country feel it but cannot identify the source of the pain. It steadily grows while workers' wages steadily shrink. Our wages as American workers have stagnated and actually shrunk in spending power since the 1970s once the world labor market was opened through "free trade." In Michigan where I live our public schools are operating in an atmosphere of scarcity. The public infrastructure of roads and bridges is crumbling around us and we struggle to maintain it. The interest each person has to pay on the national debt each year out of our personal federal income taxes is not only hurting us as individuals, but our payments are only paying the interest, while the debt's principal amount grows. The principal of the debt has grown from 6 to 9 trillion in the last 7 years. Does this huge military budget priority make sense to you in this day and age? We are still spending like we are in a world war.

The United States government is now working to control outer space through the U.S. Space Command, yes the Space Command. Is this new to you? It was to me. Here are some defining statements from the *Vision 2020* of the U.S. Space Command.

> The globalization of the world economy will also continue, with a widening between "haves" and "have-nots . . ." Just as land dominance, sea control, and air superiority is emerging as an essential element of battlefield success and future warfare . . . The emerging synergy of space superiority with land, sea, and air superiority, will lead to full spectrum dominance . . .

Does this sound like Vikings talking? It represents the embedded military dominant attitude toward the world and now, outer space.

Huge Amount Of Hoarded Wealth In America

In a world where many want wealth, those that hoard it must protect it with weapons. This has always been the way. Do we have such a large military because we as a people or a small segment of our population have such a disproportionate amount of the world's wealth? The expenditure of vast amounts of tax money is only one of the many costs of supporting a large military.

Let's look at the wealth distribution within our country. The estimated total net worth of U.S. citizens is $42,389,200,000,000.00; that's about 42.4 trillion dollars. The CIA website says there are currently around 151 million workers including the unemployed in the population of the U.S. If this wealth were divided equally among all workers, we would each control around $286,413.00 in assets, not income but net worth. Each husband and wife would be worth over a half a million dollars. But the wealth is not distributed equally in our culture nor has it ever been.

It is significant that in 2007 the top 1% of the population controls around 38% of the wealth of this country. The top 10% (as rated by wealth) of the population controls 71% of the wealth while the top 40% of the population controls 95.3% of the wealth. That means that the bottom 60% of the population controls 4.7% of the wealth. Even in the bottom 60% of the population or 88.8 million workers, if each had an equal share, a person would control an average of $23,867.00. While under these circumstances the top 10% or 14.8 million workers would each control a little over 2 million dollars.

There are trends about shifts in wealth of the population being monitored by groups like United For Fair Economy. Since the early 1980s, wealth has been shrinking for the bottom 40% of the population and growing strongly for the top 1% (1.48 million workers) of the population. According to Edward Wolfe who has studied these trends, the household net worth of the bottom 40% has dropped 76% since 1983 and the net worth of the top 1% has grown 42%. The net worth of households in the middle has grown 10 to 20%. Real wages have shrunk for most workers in the U.S. since 1980 while the top managers' share of the wealth has skyrocketed. In 1980, the average CEO made 42 times the average worker yearly pay. In 2001, the average U.S. worker made $26,764.00 and the average U. S. CEO made 11 million dollars or 411 times the average worker's wage. Whose wages are truly driving up the expenses of the product in an unrealistic way, if you want to consider the CEO a worker? Is it any wonder that the common people feel the stress of the times as their spending power shrinks? The working people within a family have to work more hours to meet the needs of the household, with prices for the basic necessities rising, and health care harder to obtain while the Federal Government seeks control in outer space and hopes to colonize Mars.

Slavery's Effect On The Legacy Of Inherited Wealth

Most of the hoarded wealth in this country is actually inherited through family legacies. The hoarding of wealth in this country and the methods employed to accumulate wealth have had many consequences; some old, some long term. In America we still suffer from the effects of slavery. We are also unique within the group of post-English colonies, since we have the descendants of a huge population of African slaves. While my ancestors were working to pay for the ranch or farm, African-American ancestors were stolen by force from their native countries and cultures then used to create wealth for others. The slave traders engaged in this enterprise gained wealth and the people who bought slaves used them without paying for their labors also gained wealth. The Africans were mistreated and exploited in this country for economic gain but they also suffered because of the ignorant prejudicial theories of racial superiority held by the Euro-Americans and inferiority attributed to the African races by members of the dominant culture. Slave owners created their wealth by not fairly paying Africans for their labor, and sustained their wealth by keeping slaves in perpetual bondage through acts of violence or threats of violence. The slave owners who held large numbers of slaves lived lavish lifestyles from the exploitation of these African people and their descendants. The attitudes of violence and the old racist beliefs that supported the so-called institution of slavery still exist for some people in this country. Those who gained the wealth including George Washington and Thomas Jefferson may be long gone but the legacy of suffering for slave descendants remains to this day while the legacy of wealth they helped to create remains among many of the descendants. African-Americans are still struggling to gain equality within our culture.

Growth Of Private Military Contractors

Chalmers Johnson wrote about the recent growth of private military contractors such as Haliburton, Brown and Root, Military Professional Resources, Inc., DynCorp, Science Applications International Corporation, and many others. Their trade organization is the International Peace Operations Association. The Pentagon hires corporations like these to train foreign military, for foreign protection of personnel, and to build and maintain foreign military bases. These companies are making a lot of money and the revenue to pay them comes from the taxpayers of the United States of America. For example, Camp Bondsteel, a new military base in Yugoslavia costs approximately $180 million a year to operate and it is maintained by Brown and Root, whose employees clean the barracks, cook the food, do the laundry, provide the electricity and water services. There is a proposed oil pipeline that will pass through the neighborhood of this base. The AMBO Trans-Balkan pipeline will pump Caspian basin oil. It appears that this long term American military base is to protect this future oil pipeline. Do you think that oil pipeline will supply oil only to American people? When our country builds one of these overseas bases we almost never give it up.

Creating Enemies With Our Foreign Military Activities

We have been building military bases all across the south side of the Persian Gulf. Our presence there along with our cash and weapons support for Israel has generated much resentment among the Arab people. Our deployment of thousands of American military forces to Saudi Arabia, the site of Islam's two most sacred sites increased their resentment. Chalmers Johnson wrote:

> The permanent deployment of American soldiers, sailors, and airmen whose culture, lifestyles, wealth, and physical appearance guarantee conflicts with the peoples who live in the Middle East, is irrational in terms of any cost-benefit analysis. In fact, given the widespread political unrest and a strong revival of militant Islam, the United States seems inexplicably intent on providing future enemies with enough grievances to do us considerable damage. It may be that the ultimate causes of twenty first century mayhem in the Middle East are American militarism and imperialism—that is, our empire of bases itself.

The philosophy of *Osama bin Ladin* is an example of the hatred and resentment brought about through our militarism in the Middle East. He made a speech directed to the American people shortly before the 2004 Presidential election. *Aljazeera* published it on the web Monday November 1, 2004. In order to understand the mind of bin Ladin and those who follow him, and perhaps why they follow him, I've excerpted part of his speech:

Praise be to Allah who created the creation for his worship and commanded them to be just and permitted the wronged one to retaliate against the oppressor in kind. To proceed:

Peace be upon he who follows the guidance: People of America this talk of mine is for you and concerns the ideal way to prevent another Manhattan, and deals with the war and its causes and results. So, I shall talk to you about the story behind those events and shall tell you truthfully about the moments in which the decision was taken, for you to consider.

I say to you, Allah knows that it had never occurred to us to strike the towers. But after it became unbearable and we witnessed the oppression and tyranny of the American/Israeli coalition against our people in Palestine and Lebanon, it came to my mind.

The events that affected my soul in a direct way started in 1982 when America permitted the Israelis to invade Lebanon and the American Sixth Fleet helped them in that. This bombardment began and many were killed and injured and others were terrorized and displaced.

I couldn't forget those moving scenes, blood and severed limbs, women and children sprawled everywhere. Houses destroyed along with their occupants and high rises demolished over their residents, rockets raining down on our home without mercy.

The situation was like a crocodile meeting a helpless child, powerless except for his screams. Does the crocodile understand a conversation that doesn't include a weapon? And the whole world saw and heard but it didn't respond.

In those difficult moments many hard-to-describe ideas bubbled in my soul, but in the end they produced an intense feeling of rejection of tyranny, and gave birth to a strong resolve to punish the oppressors.

And as I looked at those demolished towers in Lebanon, it entered my mind that we should punish the oppressor in kind and that we should destroy towers in America in order that they should taste some of what we tasted and so that they be deterred from killing our women and children.

And that day, it was confirmed to me that oppression and the intentional killing of innocent women and children is a deliberate American policy. Destruction is freedom and democracy, while resistance is terrorism and intolerance.

This means the oppressing and embargoing to death of millions as Bush Sr. did in Iraq in the greatest mass slaughter of children mankind has ever known, and it means the throwing of millions of pounds of bombs and explosives at millions of children—also in Iraq—as Bush Jr. did, in order to remove an old agent and replace him with a new puppet to assist in the pilfering of Iraq's oil and other outrages . . . .

And the same goes for your allies in Palestine. They terrorize the women and children, and kill and capture the men as they lie sleeping with their families on the mattresses, that you may recall that for every action, there is a reaction.

We go about the world creating enemies. The CIA has been behind many covert operations to influence regimes in countries all over the world where our corporate powers want some resource or control. Our government, during the Eisenhower presidency, sponsored the overthrow of democratically elected Iranian Prime Minister *Mohammad Mossadeq*. The CIA sent Theodore Roosevelt's grandson Kermit to oversee the coup. Through these efforts the Shah of Iran was brought back to power. The royal dictator ruled the country without any form of legitimate democracy, using brutality and his secret police to control dissent for almost 20 years. The Shah gave us a better deal on the oil while we sold him a lot of weapons and other contracting ventures. He was overthrown in the late 1970s by a passionate religious revolution bringing the *Ayatullah Khomeini* to power.

In Iraq our government sponsored the revolution of the Bathist Party that eventually brought *Saddam Hussein* to power. President Reagan sent his man Donald Rumsfeld to Iraq to meet with *Saddam Hussein,* giving him money and weapons to use in the Iraq-Iran war. The people in Iran and Iraq know what we have been up to. We have also been active in South and Central America. The CIA aided in the overthrow of the elected government of Salvadore Allende in Chile, installing General Pinochet during the Nixon years. President Reagan secretly funded the Contra's in Nicaragua. These actions represent only a couple of covert actions that came from the American Presidential office.

The World Bank And The International Monetary Fund

We have two other mechanisms to promote the hoarding of wealth for our elite class in the United States and to exert control over the governments of smaller countries: The World Bank and the International Monetary Fund. These organizations were created at the end of World War II to help the European reconstruction efforts. Both organizations are tied to the U.S. Treasury and the Secretary of the Treasury. Our elite using the power of these organizations can control resources in other countries without overt violence. Huge sums of money are loaned to those countries by these agencies and by manipulating trade agreements or other internal policies regulating the control of cash flow and loans, the foreign governments are forced to follow the orders of the American bureaucrats or face financial chaos, or worse. These loans come with strings attached and are largely used for the creation of infrastructure built by U.S. contractors. The World Bank lends and the International Monetary Fund imposes the policies that give us free access to the economy and control of the financial policies of these countries. Countries giving in to this pressure from these huge banking organizations become *structurally adjusted.* These indebted countries cut social programs like health care and education to free up money to pay the debts. They may also sell off public utilities and natural resources to foreign investors who take the profits out of the countries.

John Perkins who was recruited by this power structure has written a fascinating book titled *Confessions of an Economic Hitman.* Coming from an Ivy League background, he was identified by the NSA (National Security Agency) and recruited to become an economic forecaster for MAIN, an engineering consulting corporation. Perkins traveled around the world for this company through the 1970s, recommending to the leaders of foreign countries the benefits of huge infrastructure projects. He worked in Indonesia, Saudi Arabia, Panama, Iran, Ecuador and Columbia. His economic forecasts justified huge electrical construction projects. The IMF and the World Bank financed many international projects he recommended. His trainer for this position with MAIN told him his job was, ". . . to encourage world leaders to become part of a vast network that promotes U.S. commercial interests. In the end, those leaders become ensnared in a web of debt that ensures their loyalty. We can draw on them whenever we desire to satisfy our political, economic, or military needs. In turn, they bolster their political positions by bringing industrial parks, power plants, and airports to their people. The owners of U. S. engineering/construction companies become fabulously wealthy."

Perkins further stated:

> U.S. intelligence agencies-including the NSA-would identify prospective EHMs (Economic Hit Men), who could then be hired by international corporations. These EHMs would never be paid by the government; instead, they would draw their salaries from the private sector. As a result, their dirty work, if exposed, would be chalked up to corporate greed rather than government policy. In addition, the corporations that hired them, although paid by government agencies and their multinational banking counterparts (with taxpayer money), would be insulated from congressional oversight and public scrutiny, shielded by a growing body of legal initiatives, including trademark, international trade, and Freedom of Information laws.
>
> McNamara became a strong advocate of a Keynesian approach to government, using mathematical models and statistical approaches to determine troop levels, allocation of funds, and other strategies in Vietnam. His advocacy of "aggressive leadership" became a hallmark not only of government managers but also of corporate executives. I see now that Robert McNamara's greatest and most sinister contribution to history was to jockey the World Bank into becoming an agent of global empire on a scale never before witnessed.
>
> Today, men and women are going into Thailand, the Philippines, Botswana, Bolivia, and every other country

where they hope to find people desperate for work. They go to these places with the express purpose of exploiting wretched people—people whose children are severely malnourished, even starving, people who live in shantytowns and have lost all hope of a better life, people who have ceased to even dream of another day. These men and women leave their plush offices in Manhattan or San Francisco or Chicago, streak across continents and oceans in luxurious jetliners, check into first-class hotels, and dine at the finest restaurants the country has to offer. Then they go searching for desperate people.

Today, we still have slave traders. They no longer find it necessary to march into the forest of Africa looking for prime specimens who will bring top dollar on the auction blocks in Charleston, Cartegena, and Havanna. They simply recruit desperate people and build a factory to produce the jackets, blue jeans, tennis shoes, automobile parts, computer components, and thousands of other items they can sell to the market of their choosing.

These men and women think of themselves as upright. They return to their homes with photographs of quaint sites and ruins, to show their children. They attend seminars where they pat each other on the back and exchange tidbits of advice about dealing with the eccentricities of customs in far-off lands. Their bosses hire lawyers who assure them that what they are doing is perfectly legal.

The old-fashioned slave trader told himself that he was dealing with a species that was not entirely human, and that he was offering them the opportunity to become Christianized. He also understood that slaves were fundamental to the survival of his own society, that they were the foundation of his economy. The modern slave trader assures himself (or herself) that the desperate people are better off earning one dollar a day that no dollars at all, and that they are receiving the opportunity to become integrated into the larger world community. She never stops to think about the larger implications of what she, her lifestyle, and the economic system behind them are doing to the world—or how they may ultimately impact her children's future.

John Perkins did a lot of work in Ecuador over a period of almost 30 years. He saw things change a lot there and much of it as a result of the work he and others like him did. They loaned Ecuador billions of dollars to hire American engineering and construction companies to build huge projects. Perkins saw the poverty level increase by 20 percent in that country which now spends almost 50 percent of its government revenues to service its debt. We currently spend over 20 percent of our taxes to service our national debt and it is still growing. See any similarities? These lost revenues rob our workers of many other benefits they could have for that money. The children of Ecuador and the USA are born and brought up to service these debts although they had no choice in matter.

In the mid 1990s, we created the World Trade Organization (WTO). The mission of the WTO is to organize all the nations of the world under the rules of our trade policies and to open markets for our corporate agri-businesses. The rules for international trade of agricultural products were made excluding Third World countries and allowed the richer nations to subsidize their farmers and impose tariffs on the poorer countries in an effort to gain this control. The WTO also protects the pharmaceutical companies of the richer nations, allowing them to maintain control of patents on medicines, seeds, and agricultural chemicals.

Long Term Costs Of The Nuclear Weapons Program

Our United States nuclear weapons program is costing our country roughly 17 billion dollars a year. There are many delayed and hidden costs associated with this nuclear weapons program. Our country is and has been the leader in this technology since World War II. We are the only country to use these weapons against human populations. Some say the dropping of the nuclear bombs at Nagasaki and Hiroshima was to shorten the war and others say it served to warn the Russians about our new nuclear weapon. We have been the driving force in the nuclear arms race and fortunes have been made on it. Here in Michigan, Consumers Power Company was coerced into building several nuclear power plants in order to provide a source of enriched uranium for the federal weapons programs. These power plants were sold to the public as a clean way to make electricity: Look no smoke. But there is one hidden cost: The spent fuel rods and other nuclear wastes must be stored in climate-controlled conditions for 25,000 years. Yes that's 25,000 years. That's a lot of responsibility to place on human beings even 1000 years from now. The nuclear waste is also toxic to all living things. We also have Strontium 99 in the Great Lakes, a byproduct of the nuclear industry. Strontium 99 is an alpha particle emitter. It has been found at three sites in the Great Lakes. If this material gets into your body from eating the fish or drinking the water your body knits it into your bones like calcium. The alpha particles it emits kill cells and are especially dangerous to bone marrow.

The fear tactic we have used carrying this "big stick" has caused many countries to try and keep up with us in the nuclear arms race. When the USSR went bankrupt, a lot of nuclear material and weapons were left unattended in some cases in less than secure locations. Our federal government is trying to control these leftover nuclear materials to keep our enemies from obtaining them and using them against us. There is a large international smuggling business in nuclear materials. Someday we may regret our leadership in this nuclear arms race and the belief in dominance through superior weaponry. It is another divider of nations.

The growth of our militarism and empire building has its costs for the American people. Chalmers Johnson named them in *The Sorrows of Empire*. He summed it up as these four sorrows:

> First, there will be a state of perpetual war, leading to more terrorism against Americans wherever they may be and a growing reliance on weapons of mass destruction among smaller nations as they try to ward off the imperial juggernaut. Second, there will be a loss of democracy and constitutional rights as the presidency fully eclipses Congress. Third, an already well-shredded principle of truthfulness will increasingly be replaced by a system of propaganda, disinformation, and glorification of war, power, and the military legions. Lastly, there will be bankruptcy, as we pour our economic resources into ever more grandiose military projects and short-change the education, health, and safety or our fellow citizens.

Living in Michigan this is what I see happening: times are getting harder for those who cannot sell themselves to the corporate system for a good paying job. Families are stressed with Mom and Dad both having to work to maintain a home and meet the needs of the family. Our manufacturing jobs that used to be good paying jobs are shipped to other countries without any thought for what those jobs meant to our families and communities. Our cities and states are hard pressed for tax revenues especially here in my home state. The economic life expectancy of the average working person is shrinking while the elite are controlling a larger share of the wealth. Money for mental health is cut and more mentally ill are ending up on the street or in prisons. Our leaders need to remember fairness instead of bottom line greed.

Eric Fromm, the great psychoanalyst made many accurate observations about our capitalist social structure and the effect upon individual characters within our system. Fromm wrote many books about his observations of human motivation. His *Art of Loving* is a treatise on the strong need to belong to the group that manifests as conformity so as not to feel alone and his book *Escape From Freedom* is a study of the fear of not belonging to the group, the same fear that fueled the growth of Nazi Germany.

His last major book analyzed our materialist culture and was titled, *To Have or To Be.* In this book he stated:

> The second psychological premise of the industrial age, that the pursuit of individual egoism leads to harmony and peace, the growth in everyone's welfare, is equally erroneous on theoretical grounds, and again its fallacy is proven by the observable data. To be an egoist refers not only to my behavior but to my character. It means: that I want everything for myself; that possessing, not sharing, gives me pleasure; that I must become more greedy because if my aim is having, I *am* more the more I *have;* that I must feel antagonistic toward all others: my customers whom I want to deceive, my competitors whom I want to destroy, my workers whom I want to exploit. I can never be satisfied, because there is no end to my wishes; I must be envious of those who have more

and afraid of those who have less. But I have to repress all these feelings in order to represent myself (to others as well as myself) as the smiling, rational, sincere, kind human being everybody pretends to be.

Another explanation is that the selfishness the system generates makes leaders value personal success more highly than social responsibility. It is no longer shocking when political leaders and business executives make decisions that seem to be to their personal advantage, but at the same time harmful and dangerous to the community. Indeed, if selfishness is one of the pillars of contemporary practical ethics, why should they act otherwise? At the same time, the general public is also so selfishly concerned with their private affairs that they pay little attention to all that transcends the personal realm.

In contemporary society the having mode of existing is assumed to be rooted in Human nature and, hence, virtually unchangeable. The same idea is expressed in the dogma that people are basically lazy, passive by nature, and that they do not want to work or to do anything else, unless they are driven by the incentive of material gain . . . or hunger . . . or the fear of punishment. This dogma is doubted by hardly anybody, and it determines our methods of education and of work. But it is little more than an expression of the wish to prove the value of our social arrangements by imputing to them that they follow the needs of human nature. To the members of many different societies of both past and present, the concept of finite human selfishness and laziness would appear as fantastic as the reverse sounds to us.

The truth is that both the having and the being modes of existence are potentialities of human nature, that our biological urge for survival tends to further the having mode, but that selfishness and laziness are not the only propensities inherent in human beings.

We human beings have an inherent and deeply rooted desire to be: to express our facilities, to be active, to be related to others, to escape the prison cell of selfishness. The truth of this statement is proven by so much evidence that a whole volume could easily be filled with it.

The human desire to experience union with others is rooted in the specific conditions of existence that characterize the human species and is one of the strongest motivators of human behavior. This human need for unity with others is experienced in many ways: in the symbiotic tie to mother, an idol, one's tribe, one's nation, one's class, one's religion, one's fraternity, one's professional organization.

In this chapter I have tried to lay the groundwork to show that war and killing is not psychologically healthy for human beings and that selfish hoarding of wealth also causes unhealthy isolation and unhealthy human relations. If these behaviors and thought patterns promote unhealthy attitudes then I would venture to say that we were not created to do or act this way. If you are Christian you may believe that it is not our Father's will for us to be this way. Killing in war and hoarding wealth and resources are dysfunctional ways of being human and according to some Native Americans, not part of our *original instructions*. Do you know the game of Monopoly? Do you know how the winner is supposed to end up with all the money and property? Our current cultural paradigm is modeled after that philosophy.

All this negativity is tiring but it needs to be brought out into the light to be seen for what it is and discussed by all people. We need to take a good hard look at what we as a culture are doing and where we are headed as a result of our age-old ways. We have the mechanisms available for change in this country but it is going to take a change of heart on the part of many people. We need to become active, putting our minds together to look for better solutions. It is time for new beginnings. It is time to cast off the old behaviors and assumptions that are clearly dysfunctional. There is enough here on this garden planet for all if we share and care for each other in healthy ways. In the next chapters I will show examples of cultures demonstrating other ways of being human that are healthier and can lead to a better world if we can but open our hearts and minds to the possibilities.

7

Long Term
Cooperative Societies

In the United States of America, we are born into a competitively structured society. We are raised to believe that competition is the norm and that competition is the healthy way, maybe even the only way to live in our competitive, consumerist society. We are taught to *get ahead* of others because the more we have the more we are admired in our cultural social structure. Our culture of competitive consumerism and seeking wealth is attractive and spreading out across the globe to other cultures. The competitive desire for trade goods by the native people began spreading here on the North American continent with the arrival of the first Europeans.

Cooperative Culture Of The Original People Of This Continent

Three hundred and fifty years ago the arrival of the Europeans to America changed or destroyed most of the original societies that existed here. Before the Mayflower landed, diseases brought by other Europeans had ravaged Native American populations along much of the East coast. The original Pilgrim settlement at Plymouth was built at the site of an abandoned, dead Native American village. Native people had been in contact with Anglo fishermen, French voyagers, or the Spanish from the south and large parts of the original population sickened and died from these contacts. As Europeans arrived in greater numbers, the Native Americans along the coasts were pushed from their native lands into other tribes' territories.

We do know that most of the tribal societies of North America lived cooperatively among their own groups. Unlike the Europeans, they were not wealth or resource hoarders.

A *Wompanoag* elder, Medicine Story wrote about the Native Americans in his book, *Return to Creation*:

> It is necessary to confront a few myths that are propagated by schools, books, periodicals, motion pictures, and television. It is taught, and most people believe, that the indigenous people of North America were savage, brutal, warlike, hostile to strangers and cruel to each other. I call that the Big Lie, or turning the truth into its opposite.
>
> In actuality, the people of this continent were among the most pacific, gentle and friendly people to be found on the planet. Our people welcomed the visitors and treated them with courtesy and respect. Hospitality was and continues to be one of the strongest customs of native people. It was only when the visitors began to take

slaves and burn villages and steal land and dishonor their treaties that the natives began to suspect their guests' true intentions.

But what about all those Indian wars we always hear about? Well in the first place, if you try right now to remember all the Indian nations with a warlike reputation, how many can you count? Mohawk, Huron, Sioux, Apache, Comanche. Perhaps Cheyenne, Arapaho, Crow, Blackfoot. Maybe you can you'll come up with a dozen. Two dozen at the most, if you've read a lot. Very often these nations got that reputation after being attacked by the European invaders and pushed into the territories of other nations.

In North America there were about five hundred different tribes, and the vast majority lived totally peaceful existences with no violence or hostility towards their neighbors.

As for the ways of the so-called "warlike" nations, I think that "war" is a very misleading word in this context. "War Game" would better describe the outings of warriors in these tribes. There were raids, typically for honor, or revenge, or women, later for horses. Among most warrior societies it was considered more courageous to touch the enemy and ride away than to kill him. These skirmishes had nothing to do with greed for land. Certainly they were nothing like the wars of conquest for territory and riches, slaves and religious subjugation that were the fashion of Europe and Asia. There were no crusades in America, no wars of succession, no Hundred Years War, no Thirty Years War, no Seven Years War among native tribes. If war went longer than a day, it was too long.

The *Wampanoags* were the people who greeted and took pity on the *Aenglish* people who arrived aboard the Mayflower. They were the Native Americans who provided the food for the first "Thanksgiving." The original people of this continent had no system of private land ownership. Tribal groups shared the land resources. They worked gardens together and shared food resources. In many native cultures such as the *Kwakiutl* on the North American continent, the individuals who gave away the most wealth were the most respected. This is the opposite of our culture where those who are able to hoard the most wealth are held in highest social esteem.

The European trade goods, especially guns and alcohol, were sought by many of the original people of this continent. The need for these new trade items became a powerful advantage for the European traders who exploited this need among the Native Americans. For example, beaver fur was desired by the Europeans to be made into fancy felt hats in the markets of Europe. The *Iroquois* beaver hunters of New York and Canada who traded for guns and other trade items very early with the Dutch drove whole tribes from their lands while they hunted beaver in the territory of other natives. These aggressive Native American hunters quickly depleted beaver from one territory, and moved on into new hunting grounds. They pushed the native people out of Lower Michigan where I live, over into Wisconsin in the late 1600s, chasing the game that provided them with guns, rum, and other goods. The desire for these material goods destroyed the cooperative spirit among many of the native people.

The Europeans arrived, colonized, dominated and destroyed the native cultures in America. There are very few examples of organized, non-violent, cooperative societies remaining in this hemisphere. Two cultures did survive: the *Hopi* in our American Southwest are a good example and the *Kogi* of Columbia. Take off your Viking filters and look at these societies. These native peoples live in balance with their surrounding natural world, as they have for thousands of years. They live in stone houses, cultivate crops, weave clothes, and enjoy natural lives in cooperation with the natural world and each other.

Hopi Of The American Southwest

Much has been written about the *Hopi* who live in *pueblo* areas of the American Southwest. During my travels around this continent, I had an opportunity to visit with a *Hopi* member of the Eagle Clan who told me about his people. We had been to Mesa Verde National Monument visiting the stone ruins there, an area that left me with a lot of questions. The park rangers who guide tours told us of the *Anasazi* who built the cliff dwellings and then disappeared. My *Hopi* acquaintance said his ancestors had built the mysterious dwellings in the National Park and that some *Hopi* people had tried to return to these cliff dwellings at the beginning of the 20th Century, not knowing the area had become a National Park.

The *Hopi* believe that after the great flood that cleansed the last world, they arrived at what they call this world. The creator told them that they must travel to the four corners of this continent before they permanently settled one area. They were to do this to cleanse from themselves any social dysfunction they brought with them from the last world. The *Hopi* man told me that they came to the place they eventually settled and decided to stay there because it was a place that had nothing anyone would want to come and take. Largely desert, it was not desirable farmland. This would help them avoid a lot of conflict. He told me that only through their faith could they live in such a place because it took an active prayer life to bring the rain and grow their sacred corn, the sustenance of life.

There is a legend that interests me about their pilgrimage around this continent. When each of the Hopi tribal groups completed their journey to the four corners of this continent and returned they were asked a question. The question was, "Did you use your power against other human beings?" If they answered yes they could not enter the main settlement.

The Hopi have a very active, secretive religious life with complicated ceremonies to work with nature and its forces to keep their world in balance. It is through cooperative action among themselves and the greater natural world that has allowed them to exist in this place for over 1000 years.

Kogi Of South America

The *Kogi* are not well known to most people outside of their homeland. These native people live largely as they did during pre-Columbian times, on a mountain near Santa Marta, Columbia. This mountain provides their livelihood and their safety. The people are mostly farmer/gardeners, weavers, stone workers, and turkey farmers. Several small farms are individually worked and members of the tribe perform cooperative work for the community. The *Kogi* escaped extermination or subjugation because they lived where the Spaniard's horses could not easily climb up to their homeland and they did not have enough gold to justify the chase by other means. They are the remnants of the *Tairona* culture, a name given to them by the Spanish.

Alan Ereira, a BBC filmmaker went to Columbia to work on a film about Spanish gold. He found out about the *Kogi* when he filmed some of their gold relics in a museum there.

Ereira produced a documentary and wrote a book about them. The book is titled, *The Elder Brothers.* It took Ereira several years to work out a visit with the *Kogi* people. He had to nego- tiate with the *Kogi* and the Columbian government. The *Kogi,* who refer to themselves as the Elder Brothers, have a message for the rest of us who they call the Younger Brothers.

The *Kogi* people are descendents of a very organized self- sufficient, ancient culture, living on a mountain that rises 19,000 feet above the coastline of Columbia. At one time there were over a half million people in the cultural group, interde- pendent and living in harmony with the ecosystem there. Each group, whether they lived near the seashore or high in the mountains, produced something for the entire group. Those living at sea level produced salt and caught fish. Further up the mountain they grew cotton and wove clothes.

At the base of the *Kogi's* mountain, the Spanish Conquis- tadors arrived in 1525 A.D. and founded Santa Marta, Colum- bia. For the first 70 years after the Spaniard's arrival, the *Kogi* and the Spanish co-existed. The Spanish demanded gold and the *Kogi* paid them. When the coastal people ran out of gold and could no longer pay, those living at higher elevations paid for them so their community organization could go on. In 1595 A.D. when the Spanish demanded that the *Kogi* become members of the Roman Catholic Church they rebelled, and in the short fight that ensued the survivors escaped up the moun- tain where their descendants live today.

The *Kogi's* daily lives and their larger society are organ- ized around mostly a male priesthood. They are called *Mamas* and they are involved in guiding everyday life, believing it is their job to keep the earth in balance so that life can exist in a healthy way on this planet. A *Mama* is selected at birth through divination. The selected infant is raised in a very strict way for the first seven years of his life high atop the mountain. The child is kept in the dark for the first few years of life. The *Kogi* believe this will keep the child more in touch with the world of spirit where it had previously existed before birth. The training remains rigorous until adulthood. Meditation performed high on the mountain is a very important part of the *Mama's* life. The *Kogi* believe the creator to be the Great Mother who through her thoughts creates all life, first in spirit form and then in physical form. The *Kogi Mamas* have a message for us the *younger brothers*. Alan Eriera brought this message to us in his book printed in 1992:

> We are the Elder Brothers.
> We have not forgotten the old ways.
> How could I say that I do not know how to dance?
> We still know how to dance.
> We have forgotten nothing.
> We know how to call in the rain.
> If it rains too hard we know how to stop it.
> We call the summer.
> We know how to bless the world and make it flourish.
>
> But now you are killing the Mother.
> The Younger Brother, all he thinks about is plunder.
>
> The Mother looks after him too, but he does not think.
>
> He is cutting into her flesh.
> He is cutting off her arms.
> He is cutting off her breasts.
> He takes out her heart. He is killing the heart of the world.
>
> When the final darkness falls, everything will stop.
> The fires, the benches, the stones, everything.
> All the world will suffer.

When they kill all the Elder Brothers then they too will be
finished.
We will all be finished.

What would they think if all the Mamas die?
Would they think, well? So what? Or what would they think?

If that happened and all the Mamas died, and there was no
one doing our work, well the rain wouldn't fall from the sky.
It would get hotter and hotter from the sky, and trees
    wouldn't grow,
And crops wouldn't grow.

Or am I wrong and they would grow anyway?

Alan spent a good deal of time with these people and they
saw him as someone who could get their message out to the
greater world. He commented upon their observations and
feelings. They realized the problem of global warming before
most of us knew about the concept. Alan stated:

> The *Mamas* know that this process has begun. I still did
> not know how they knew, or what precisely had so
> frightened them, but the constant mention of water was
> obviously significant. Over and over again they warned
> of heat and drought, and the end of life. This is not a
> game: it is the most important thing in the world, for
> them and for us.

The *Kogi* depend upon the ice caps and snowfall high on
their mountain for the melting waters that rush downward and
irrigate their crops. They have seen their mountain begin to
dry up as the ice caps shrink. Sound familiar? The *Kogi* see
themselves as gardeners with original, ancient instructions to
take care of this garden.

Ereira spoke about this belief:

> The Sierra, as I heard about it and experienced it in the company of the *Mamas*, appeared to be the garden of Eden, a heart of the world containing the whole of the world. And here, I was told, the Mother's offspring, her male child *Serankua*, created humans. They were made to look after the world, to care for everything in it. Animals and plants were placed not under their dominion but in their care.

These people have stone houses with thatched roofs, a complicated system of stone walking roads, cotton cloth, and a balanced culture that once numbered a half a million people living in harmony with their mountain. They see changes occurring in the environment, caused by the inharmonious actions of other cultures. Their message is for us to wake up and stop destroying our world by chasing after wealth.

Amish Of North America

The Amish, a Christian group, live together among the larger population of the United States. Originally, they came to America in the 1700s at the invitation of William Penn who created a religious freedom experiment in what is now Pennsylvania. There are about 130,000 living in the U.S. and Canada now, but the vast majority live in the U.S. The Amish, an offshoot of Swiss Mennonites who broke away from the Mennonites in 1693 followed the leadership of Jacob Amman. He believed in practicing stricter observances of interpreted Christianity than the original Mennonites. Amman particularly wanted stricter shunning, the practice of not speaking to or eating with those who have transgressed moral practices. For example, shunning would have been invoked if someone consorted with the English nonbelievers. The Amish as a Christian Sect rarely allow converts. They do not try to recruit members from the outside world because that would be consorting with those who are shunned.

The Amish live a strict life apart from the larger culture that they call the "English." They are governed by groups of their elder lay ministers and they speak mainly German. Four points that define them are:

1. They are followers of Jesus Christ through the New Testament
2. They live in Peace with God and with fellow believers
3. They live a life of simplicity and mutual service
4. They believe in separation from the world

The Amish place important emphasis on child training. Their children attend Amish schools whose primary goals are teaching humility and cooperation whereas we teach competition and pride in achievement at public and most private schools. They have won the right *not* to educate their young past the 8th grade. They pay taxes like all U.S. citizens but they do not pay or participate in our Social Security system because they believe in taking care of their old people and they do that. They do not serve in our armed services but they will serve in a civilian way.

Cooperative Culture Of Ladakh

In my search for examples of cooperative cultures I found an interesting article by Helena Norberg-Hodge about what she witnessed living in an area of India north of the Himalaya's called *Ladakh*. It is a large isolated area of land encompassing 40,000 square miles with 120,000 people living in it. A road was built into this area in the 1960s and Norberg-Hodge was one of the first Westerners to arrive in this province in the early 1970s. She described *Ladakh* as a land situated at a very high altitude and very dry because the rain does not make it over the mountains. The people use the glacial melt streams to irrigate their crops. They have food enough to satisfy their needs but little other resources. Their culture was one of cooperation and sharing rather than competition and hoarding. Helena lived in *Ladakh* for 11 years and witnessed cultural change as tourists and trade goods came into this region along the new road.

Ladakh has mainly a Tibetan Buddhist population but nearly half the people are Muslim. At the time of Norberg-Hodge's arrival the people of *Ladakh* lived as they had been living for hundreds of years within an interdependent agricultural based economy. The growing season is short, about four months and that is the busy time. The balance of the year is spent feeding the animals, making music, and enjoying life. Norberg-Hodge wrote:

> There is a high level of co-operation between all members of the society, with little distinction between rich and poor, male and female, old and young. Roles are very flexible. Women do some jobs more than men and vice versa: but rigid distinctions are rare. There is very little specialization, and as a result, work is rarely monotonous and boring. Everyone knows how to plant, how to build houses, how to make music, how to spin. Crime of any sort is so uncommon as to be virtually nonexistent. You can walk alone at night, without the slightest worry.

Even after getting drunk at parties people do not get aggressive.

Co-operation rather than competition lies at the foundation of *Ladakhi* society. It can be seen in all spheres of life; from the sharing of household tasks and rotational shepherding to the interaction between children. One interesting observation that I have made in this regard is that in *Ladakh*, children are never segregated into age groups. Instead, they spend their entire lives constantly surrounded by and interacting with people of all ages.

Perhaps the most important characteristic of the *Ladakhis* that forced me to rethink my beliefs about human nature is the remarkable *joie de vivre* of the people. At first I thought that the *Ladakhis* smiled a lot and appeared very happy, but surely underneath they were just like all human beings—with problems of jealousy, anger and depression. But after some years of living with them, I started realizing that all that laughter was connected to a deep sense of peace and contentedness.

During the 11 years Norberg-Hodge lived among the *Ladakhis,* she witnessed change in the culture with the advent of tourists and trade goods from the West. She noted:

This is the heartbreaking change I am now seeing: the people's perception of themselves is changing dramatically. Because of the very distorted picture of the outside world that they are gaining through contact with tourists, young people are beginning to think of themselves as poor and deprived. Since *Ladakh* first opened up, there has been an annual invasion of wealthy Westerners (as many as fifteen thousand a year). The Westerners are rich, and can travel thousands of miles for pleasure. They come for a few days, and spend perhaps 100 (pounds) a day. In a subsistence economy, where basic needs are met without money, this is as if Martians would come to Bristol and spend 50,000 (pounds) a day. 100 (pounds) is what a family in *Ladakh* might spend in a year (only using money for luxuries, as they do).

The impact on the young is disastrous; they suddenly feel that their parents and grandparents must be stupid to be working and getting dirty, when everyone else is having such a good time—spending vast quantities of money traveling and not working. So they get the impressions that if you are modern, you simply don't work; the machines do it for you. Understandably, the effect is that they try to prove that they are not part of this primitive bunch of farmers, but part of the new elegant modern world, with jeans, sunglasses, a radio, a motorbike. It is not that the blue-jeans (often uncomfortable) are intrinsically of interest; they are symbols of the modern world. Similarly, cinema films give the impression that racing around in sports cars shooting people—that violence—is modern and admirable.

All these things (trade goods) require money to be purchased so the young have to move to the cities where there are jobs if money is what they want. But all the other problems that accompany the struggle for trade goods are in the cities. There they find a modern educational system where they spend a lot of time learning things typical of public schools. This will further break down their traditional society because they do not learn what they have learned at home for hundreds of years, the traditional skills that have ensured their survival in this land of scarcity. Here is an example of the seductive power for material things that binds us all to the grid of trade goods.

I have sought out a few stories of existing, working human societies that are cooperative and nonviolent in their nature to show that they can and do exist. The people in them do not get up to go to work in a square concrete building where they look out the window wishing they were outside rather than inside. They don't work long days in drudgery doing some piece of work to get money to buy what they need. They produce what they need in much less time than we do working our 50-hour weeks. They do not hoard wealth or resources and protect it with armed guards or weapons. They spend a lot more time in the sun and fresh air. Cultures that do not hoard wealth or build sophisticated weapons systems are discredited by our culture whose members do hoard wealth and build expensive weapons systems. The examples of these societies I have shown you have a solid spiritual foundation that is the corner-stone and binder of their societies.

Darwin: Competition And Variation

Science has been used by Western society to support unhealthy competition. We are taught that natural selection is the larger order of life on Earth. In the world of large creatures that is somewhat true. Humanity is part of this web of life being a large mammal but we also function quite differently here. First, let's look at Charles Darwin.

Charles Darwin was born into a family of scientists and doctors in England around 1800. He had a hard time finding his fit into that world as he loved the world outdoors and hated the formal education of the time. His grandfather, Erasmus Darwin had actually dabbled with the ideas of evolution in the time when the popular idea was that God created the world in the last 6000 years. Darwin's love of the outdoors and the in-fluence of certain professors led him to become a naturalist. He was offered an opportunity to travel around the world collecting species of plants, insects, and animals aboard an English naval vessel when he graduated in the 1830s. Through this travel and his keen eye for observing the natural world, including geology, he got to see a lot of variation and evidence of the ancient ever-changing Earth. Darwin deduced his theory of evolution from these observations.

Darwin wrote many books about his observations and they were revolutionary at the time. The literalists of the Bible would not accept that the Earth was older than 6,000 years old or that living forms slowly evolved over a much longer time period. Darwin noted that parents produce a variety of offspring, each different somewhat than the other. He called this *variation*. These variations that survived natural selection in, " . . . the great battle for life," lived to reproduce and pass on that variation on to future generations. Evolution then is the theory of a long trail of variations that survive to reproduce their traits in the world over millions of years which in turn bring about the many varied forms of life upon Earth.

Charles Darwin did not originate the saying "the survival of the fittest." It is a judgmental phrase coined by an English sociologist of the day named Herbert Spencer. Spencer applied Darwin's theories to human society using his cultural prejudices. The capitalists and militarists of the day took up the theme as justification for competitive capitalism and military domination. They used Darwin's observations to project evolution to mean progress and justification for a system of competitive domination producing winners and losers. Darwin clearly stated his observations in scientific terms and was humble enough to also state the limits of his knowledge.

There are many living expressions of life on this planet that are basically still unexplained simply by the Theory of Evolution. When these were brought up to Darwin as criticisms of his theory he looked at possibilities but still had no real explanations. One question that haunted him was how does a nerve become light sensitive and develop into the complex human eye. Other questions pertained to the arrangement of flower petals, leaves, and cells.

There is also a great void on the actual cause of variation. He stated in his book *The Origin of the Species*:

> I have hitherto sometimes spoken as if variations were due to chance. This, of course is a wholly incorrect expression, but serves to acknowledge plainly our ignorance of the cause of each particular variation . . .
>
> . . . the greater variability of species having wider ranges than those with restricted ranges, leads to the conclusion that variability is generally related to the conditions of life to which each species has been exposed during several successive generations.
>
> In one sense the conditions of life may be said, not only to cause variability, either directly or indirectly, but likewise to include natural selection, for the conditions determine whether this or that variety shall survive.
>
> Our ignorance of the laws of variation is profound.

A Cooperative Web Of Life On Earth

Looking at the large picture of life on Earth and its organization some scientists have new conclusions based upon the data provided by better microscopes and digital technology. They see self-regulating, cooperative systems functioning together producing the living world and environment that we see. Evolutionary biologist Elisabet Sahtouris in her book, *Earthdance* summarizes this growing hypothesis based upon what has been observed with newer technology and a growing knowledge of microbiology and DNA. Elisabet Sahtouris discussed in her book what has been termed Gaia:

> The new view of our Gaian Earth in evolution shows, on the contrary, an intricate web of cooperative mutual dependency, the evolution of one scheme after another that harmonizes conflicting interests.
>
> The patterns of evolution show us the creative maintenance of life in all its complexity. Indeed nature is more suggestive of a mother juggling resources to ensure each family member's welfare as she works out differences of interest to make the whole family a cooperative venture, than of a rational engineer designing perfect machinery that obeys unchangeable laws.

Sahtouris pointed out that after the Earth was formed, life has existed for 3.7 billion years. For 2 billion years that life was single-celled bacteria of three different types. She calls them bubblers, blue greens, and breathers. First there were the bubblers who through the fermentation process broke up certain molecules that surrounded them, to create food and energy. In the early sea covered with a thin atmosphere of mainly carbon dioxide, the single-celled creatures multiplied. When the early resources grew scarce some strains of these early single-celled creatures developed a new way to produce the food energy they needed: photosynthesis. This photosynthesis seemed like a wonderful development but it created a waste gas that was deadly to the bubblers: *oxygen.* Sahtouris called these new single-celled creatures that photosynthesized the blue greens. The blue greens multiplied and pumped the oxygen and nitrogen into the developing atmosphere. The bubblers had to hide from the oxygen for survival, as it was a deadly gas to them. The blue greens were a very successful bacterial form that multiplied in many variations. A third kind of single-cell bacteria now developed, one that used the oxygen in its process of creating food energy and discharged carbon dioxide gas as waste. Sahtouris called these creatures, the breathers. As time passed, it seems that some aggressive little breathers started invading the larger blue greens to get at the rich food molecules they held. They began eating the blue greens from the inside out. This would have lead to the destruction of the blue greens species but they learned to cooperate. The blue greens began living with the breathers inside, exchanging oxygen for the energy the breathers were creating. This is the beginning of more complex cells that exist today using cooperation. As time went on more complex cooperation was developed among these early life forms until we have the complex eukaryote cells (with nucleus) of today.

Intelligent Genetic Mutation

In her book, Sahtouris told of amazing demonstrations of intelligence these basic creatures exhibited in earlier times and now. First of all, it is known now that bacteria can mutate its own DNA in relation to conditions in its external environment. Accidental genetic mutation is not the only source of variation. Intelligence is also involved in the process. Bacteria communicate with each other by coming close to one another and each one thins its cell walls whereby they can exchange small bits of DNA. When bacteria read each other's DNA, it is a learning process. They examine dead bacteria in this manner to find out what has happened. This type of bacterial investigation explains their resistance to antibiotics. They create communities with structures and move about resources such as nuclear materials.

Sahtouris wrote:

Every living creature of Earth not a bacterium itself evolved from these nucleated cells, meaning that every living being of every kingdom of life beyond monera is made of the same basic kind of nucleated cell. Biologists call this superkingdom of cells, which includes the protest, fungus, plant, and animal kingdoms, *eukaryotes* (pronounced you-carry-oats).

Eukaryote cells, as we said, are on the average a thousand times bigger than prokaryotes, with a thousand times more DNA. They are in many ways as complex as human cities, or the bacterial colony cities described earlier. Until recently, scientists saw the nucleus as a computer behaving like an authoritarian dictatorship, containing all the information necessary to run the cell and sending out 'top-down' command and control orders for what is to be built, produced, carried about, or otherwise done. Now it seems that the governing of cells is more decentralized—that the whole cell governs itself, using the nucleus as an information resource center . . .

With ever more powerful microscopes, moving picture microscopy and animation techniques, we begin to understand how busy and lively, how complicated and amazing, life is inside such cells. But what we see leaves much to be learned about how it is all organized to function so smoothly. Even structurally we are still discovering things of major importance in cells. For example, until recently we thought cells were bags of jelly-like substance with the nucleus and organelles suspended within the jelly. Then to their surprise, microbiologist Don Ingber discovered that cells have an internal architecture not unlike our bone and muscle systems—

A huge new development is that understanding that nuclear DNA is reorganized in response to changes within and beyond the cell, that the entire cell, including its membrane or wall, is a creative autopoietic system. An autopoietic system is self-producing and self –maintaining. It must constantly change or renew itself in order to stay the same. Your body renews most of its cells within each seven years of your life, for instance, and its molecules are turned over even faster. No mechanism can do this, because it does not invent and build itself, it must be invented, built, and repaired by external beings.

All the cells of our own bodies (not counting the myriad bacteria living on and within us) are eukaryote cells, but we are just beginning to understand their evolution from ancient bacterial cooperatives.

1993 Nobel Prize winning biologists Philip Sharp and Richard Roberts discovered that genes are broken into modules that can be reshuffled by *spliceosomes* referred to as a cell's 'editors' because they ship out inappropriate DNA sequences occurring between meaningful 'words.' Some of these modules are apparently shared by different genes, enabling evolution to proceed much faster than it could have if the old models held true. The picture emerging is consistent with the description given here of evolution as an intelligent process, rather than an accidental mechanical process. Sharp, in fact, speaks of a splicesome as *knowing* where to cut and where to splice.

The DNA plans and composition of our own cells are of course, unique to humans and differ from those of frog or fern cells, bacterial or Bactrian camel cells. Among the parts of our cells outside their nuclei are large numbers of tiny things that produce ATP energy currency. These cell parts have long been understood as little mechanisms for burning food molecules with oxygen to produce the cell's energy. But with rising interest in and understanding of DNA, biologists made a very strange discovery: that these little machines have their own DNA, the coded plans of which are quite different from those of the nuclear DNA.

How could cell parts be of different species than the creature made of those cells?

Clues soon turned up. However different this DNA is from the nuclear DNA, it was found to be rather like some other DNA that biologists knew about—the DNA of bacteria quite like the breathers that evolved billions of years ago! At the time this was discovered, the story of bacterial cooperation in the evolution of eukaryotes was still unknown. Now that we know it, scientists are finding as many as a thousand different kinds of DNA outside the nucleus of a single cell.

The idea of cell *symbiosis*—the origin of eukaryotes as prokaryotes living together in cooperatives—had been proposed independently by a German, an American, and a Russian biologist around the turn of the century. . . . But biologists, who were trained to see living things as put together from mechanical parts, could not see cell parts as creatures in themselves.

Thus the symbiosis theory was ignored until Lynn Margulis an American microbiologist who became James Lovelock's partner in developing the Gaia hypothesis, revived it and produced a great deal of evidence to support it.

After much work, Margulis and others have shown that these energy-producing cell parts really are descendants of the ancient breather bacteria that came to live inside larger prokaryote cells, cooperating in building the first eukaryote cells. Luckily, teams of biologists working to unravel the ancient mysteries of cell symbiosis have found many clues in the behavior of today's bacteria. Rather vicious breathers can still be found drilling their way into other bacteria to reproduce there and eat the host bacteria from the inside. In the Tennessee laboratory of Kwang Jeon, protist hosts so invaded, learned to tolerate and then to cooperate with their invaders in a mutually dependent relationship that brought about a new type of creature. Surprisingly, this replay of the ancient evolutionary shift from outright aggression to full cooperation happened in only a few years' time.

Today, we find the descendants of the ancient breathers living and multiplying in the cells of every kind of protist, fungus, plant, and animal. It's high time we knew them by name. They are *mitochondria*—pronounced, mite-o-KON-dree-a—a word that comes from the Greek meaning 'thread grains,' because under a microscope they look like tiny grain hulls packed full of thread.

Using the oxygen we breathe, mitochondria make all the energy our bodies need to keep going and to repair themselves. Without mitochondria we could not lift a finger. In fact, it is these swarms of ancient bacteria, working night and day in all our cells that keep us alive.

Our cells are each a complicated living system within a larger complicated living system, our bodies. Biologists see these cellular systems working cooperatively within themselves, all parts contributing to the larger function and each part able to negotiate for its individual needs with no part hoarding more than what it needs for survival. Competition is not a part of the operation. All cells operate with some form of intelligence. The scientists confirm what I have felt for a long time: the Earth and the universe are saturated with intelligence.

The larger system for example, our own bodies or the bodies of other creatures have parts that also work cooperatively to meet the needs of function and life with no part of the system hoarding or controlling resources in its interest without considering the needs of the other parts. The theory or belief in accidental genetic mutation driving the variation and development of all the beautiful and complex life on Earth is now in question. It seems that there is intelligence driving many of the genetic DNA changes that cause variation.

Examinations of the geological record showed these first single-celled creatures, bacteria lived competitively as a species before they learned to cooperate. If they had not learned cooperation they would have perished. These early microbes began changing the rock into the environment we now know. The early single-celled creatures became the bacteria and tiny creatures of today that make up most of the soil on earth. They are in the cells of all living things and make up most of the weight of living creatures. The bacteria cooperatively create the gases in the atmosphere that we breathe and those that protect us from the burning radiation. They continue to create the atmosphere daily and it somehow self- regulates to maintain the balance of oxygen that we need to live healthy lives on this planet. It is a cooperatively balanced living world, the backdrop of our lives.

So, looking at the larger and smaller framework of existence, life is only possible because of cooperative living arrangements between the smaller parts, bacteria and microbes living independently or as part of larger creatures. We are living systems within the larger living system. Sahtouris expanded upon this thought when she wrote:

> As pointed out earlier, no place on Earth today, not even the barest-looking mountaintop or the deepest part of the sea, has fewer than a thousand different species from various kingdoms—monera, protists, fungi, plants, and animals. Yet what we humans see as living things are only the largest plants and animals—beings the size of bugs and bushes and beluga whales, creatures on our own size scale. The vast majority of Earth creatures, however, continue to be microscopic monera and pro-

tists. Think once again of our rocky planet rearranging itself through chemical activity into a rich network of bacteria and environments that are good homes for bacteria. This is what most of the activity of our living planet is still all about.

She sees us as adolescent species acting like teenagers rebelling against our parents. Thinking we know much more than we do and making a great mess here. Are we ready to grow up now?

8

Jesus Of Nazareth's Teachings On Killing And The Hoarding Of Wealth

Jesus of Nazareth or Jesus the Christ is and has been the central figure in Anglo-Saxon religious life since at least the time of the *Anglo-Saxon Chronicles*. Those 10th Century writings, a chronology of historic events, reference all dates from the birth of the Christ child and intermingle Christian historic events with Anglo-Saxon tribal events. When the Anglo-Saxon leaders were initially baptized as Christians, the common people were still worshipers of *Woden*, *Thor*, and *Hearthen* (Mother Earth). The Anglo-Saxon warrior practices and devotion to power and wealth did not change. The religious ceremony, icons, and holidays were instead assimilated into the warrior leaders' lives. One thousand years later, I see the Viking mentality still at odds with the teachings of Jesus.

I have been seeking clues to the mystery of Jesus the

Christ through out my life. Growing up in a violent competitive society I felt there was something twisted with the presentation of his message in churches that supported war. His statements as presented in the New Testament are clear on the subject of killing one's fellow man and the hoarding of riches. He does not contradict himself. His teachings ring the bell of truth within my heart and it responds seeking to be of service. I quote some of the words of Jesus from my grandfather's King James Bible which illustrate his position:

Gospel of St. Matthew
Chapter 5
Verse 9: Blessed are the peacemakers for they shall be called the children of God.
Verse 21: Ye have heard that it was said by them of old time, thou shalt not kill; and whosoever shall kill shall be in danger of the judgment.
Verses 38–48: Ye have heard that it hath been said, An eye for an eye, and a tooth for a tooth But I say unto you, That ye resist not evil, But whosoever shall smite thee on thy right cheek, turn to him the other also. And if any man will sue thee at the law, and take away thy coat, let him have *thy* cloak also. And whosoever shall compel thee to go a mile, go with him twain. Give to him that asketh thee, and from him that would borrow of thee turn not thou away.

Ye have heard that it hath been said, Thou shalt love thy neighbor, and hate thine enemy.

But I say unto you, Love your enemies, bless them that curse you, do good to them that hate you, and pray for them which despitefully use you, and persecute you; That ye may be the children of your Father which is in heaven: for he maketh his sun to rise on the evil and the good, and sendeth rain on the just and on the unjust. For if ye love them which love you, what reward have ye?

Do not even the publicans do the same? And if ye salute your bretheren only, what do ye more *than others*? Do not even the publicans do so? Be ye therefore perfect, even as your Father which is in heaven is perfect.

Chapter 6
Verses 19–24: Lay not up for yourselves treasures upon earth, where moth and rust doth corrupt, and where thieves break through and steal, But lay up for yourselves treasures in heaven, where neither moth nor rust doth corrupt, and where thieves break through nor steal, For where your treasure is there will your heart be also. No man can serve two masters: for either he will hate the one, and love the other; or else he will hold to the one, and despise the other. Ye cannot serve God and mammon.

Gospel of St. Mark
Chapter 10
Verses 17–25: And when he was gone forth into the way, there came one running, and kneeling to him, and asked him Good Master, what shall I do that I may inherit eternal life? And Jesus said unto him, Why callest me good? *There is* none good but one, *that is* God. Thou knowest the commandments, Do not commit adultery, Do not kill, Do not steal, Do not bear false witness, Defraud not, Honour thy father and mother. And he answered and said unto him, Master, all these have I observed from my youth. Then Jesus beholding him loved him, and said unto him, One thing thou lackest: go thy way, sell whatsoever thou hast, and give to the poor, and thou shalt have treasure in heaven: and come take up the cross, and follow me. And he was sad at that saying, and went away grieved: for he had great possessions. And Jesus looked round about, and saith unto his disciples, How hardly shall they that have riches enter into the kingdom of God! And the disciples were astonished at his words. But Jesus answered again, and saith unto them, Children, how hard is it for them that trust in riches to enter into

the kingdom of God!

It is easier for a camel to go through the eye of a needle, than for a rich man to enter into the kingdom of God.

Gospel of St. Luke
Chapter 6
Verses 27–28: But I say unto you which hear, Love your enemies, do good to them which hate you. Bless them that curse you, and pray for them which despitefully use you.
Verse 35: But love ye your enemies, and do good, and lend, hoping for nothing again; and your reward shall be great, and ye shall be the children of the Highest: for he is kind unto the unthankful and *to* the evil.

These are the uncompromising words of Jesus we can read in the New Testament of the Holy Bible. He did not state that occasionally you have to go to war and kill if directed by King or President. Jesus clearly tells us to love one another even those who would do harm to us, not to lay up treasure on this earth and his words tell us to keep his commandments and to apply them to our lives as we walk this Earth.

It is amazing to me that the Bible representing Jesus' ministry to the people of the world has so little about his life and very few of his words in it. Thomas Jefferson took apart the New Testament and pasted the words of Jesus, printed in four languages, in his book, *The Morals of Jesus.* He is said to have stated, ". . . they gleam as jewels in a dung heap." Even in four languages it is a much smaller book.

Constantine And The Bible

I discovered, during my teen years, how the Bible came to be the book we know today. It was through the power and inspiration of the Roman Emperor Constantine, not a Christian until his deathbed conversion around 350 A.D. The scriptures included in the book we know as the Holy Bible today were assembled between 325 and 350 A.D. during the time when the Christian Church formalized its dogma and power under Constantine.

Constantine or someone in his direct family had a vision, before a battle at the Milvian Bridge, a battle that ended up consolidating his power as the Roman Emperor. The message of the vision was this: "Under one sign, conquer." Constantine instructed his soldiers to put the symbol of Christ on their shields to represent the sign seen in the vision. He won the battle and felt the vision had been part of the victory.

In 325 A.D. Constantine called the first great council of all the known Christian bishops to the city of Nicea (Constantinople) in order to clarify and consolidate standard teaching of the church. After heated debate lasting several months, the bishops could still not come to an agreement on specific points related to the nature of Jesus. There was a major split between these bishops. The majority of bishops were lead by Bishop Alexander of Alexandria and his right hand man *Athanasius*. These people had begun teaching the Trinity and the complete divinity of Jesus, that Jesus was God disguised as a man. The other side led by *Arius* also of Alexandria was teaching that Jesus was created a man and elevated to the Christ through his effort: ". . . he was vigilant and zealous in avoiding evil," to quote a letter written by Alexander while at Constantinople. An *Arian* creed was signed by 18 Bishops and presented to the council but it was torn to pieces rather than read. There is very little left of *Arius'* words because they were all torn up or burned so the major evidence is based on what was written about him. *Arius* was excommunicated during this council and his book was burned on the spot. Constantine favored Jesus as God and he supported the bishops who proposed that viewpoint.

Legitimized by the secular power of Roman Emperor Constantine, the Nicean Council concluded with the formal adoption of the viewpoint that Jesus was God, the only begotten of the Father. Constantine, the sun worshipper, invited those who would sign the creed to stay on as his guests in the celebration of his 20th year as Emperor. Those bishops who would not sign the creed were threatened with banishment. All signed. The decisions of the council and its aftermath established the precedence of a secular ruler's right to intervene in matters of Christian formal doctrine. Emperor Constantine enforced a church dogma and power structure that supported his divine privilege and the empire it sought to maintain through violence.

This council's creed made Jesus God never created but always had been and always will be. It took his freewill of choice away by making him always God. He did not become what he was through his choice or effort because he had always been God. It also changed the nature of humanity in this relationship by separating him from humanity. Humanity by the Nicean Creed has no chance of becoming like Jesus by following his path or the path he showed us. The human need only believe in this story of Jesus and his or her salvation is assured as long as the believer follows the church now deemed the mediator between man and God.

The Roman Catholic Church arose from the Nicean Council, and it became the only legal, state-sanctioned Christian religious organization for a thousand years thereafter. Constantine gave the Roman bishop wealth, power over the other bishops and an army thus creating the position that would become known as the Pope. Before this time the Bishop of Rome had no more power than any other bishop over the somewhat independent diverse congregations. Disagreements with the pronouncements of the Roman Catholic Church were deemed heresy, punishable by death. With the exception of a few scattered outposts beyond the political reach of this church, the dogma of the Roman Catholic Church became the only acceptable belief system for a citizen of the empire— though sporadic persecution of Christians did occur again under later Roman emperors. As Joseph Macchio brings forward to us Constantine declared dissenting Christian groups could no longer meet in public:

> Understand by this present statute, Novations, Valentinians, Marconionites, Paulinians, with what destructive and venomous errors, your doctrines are inextricably woven! We give you warning . . . Let none of you presume, from this time forward, to meet in congregations. To prevent this, we command that you be deprived of all the houses in which you have been accustomed to meet . . . and that these should be handed over to the Catholic Church.

The Roman Churche's Bible was assembled as a selected group of the many Hebrew, Greek, and Aramaic scriptures approved by the bishops who sponsored the creed. Constantine ordered new copies of "the scriptures" made in 331A.D. These documents were canonized as the true and only true documents of the ancient traditions and became the Holy Bible. There were numerous other writings of the time pertaining to Jesus the Christ and other Biblical figures but many were burned, hidden away or lost.

It should be pointed out that Constantine changed his

mind about *Arius* and ordered him reinstated in Alexandria when Bishop Alexander died. *Athanasius* refused Arius to enter the city. *Arius* died also at this time and after his death, his teachings became more popular and followers of the two sides began violently struggling against each other. The emperor did not claim the Christian faith for himself (beyond political purposes) by baptism until he was near death. For much of his life Constantine worshiped the sun, as his father had, in pagan fashion—hence the origins of Sunday. After his death, the shrewd statesman himself was consecrated as a pagan deity. The influence of Constantine and the secular power he wielded over the development of the early church is undeniable. The Roman Church became a religion that supported empire builders as well as humble saints.

Jesus And the Essenes

Jesus was born into the Arabic Hebrew culture in Palestine around 2030 years ago. This was a very religious culture following the Law of Moses. At this time, the Jews were a religiously fragmented people in divergent sects and they were dominated by a foreign power, the Romans. The Jewish people had written language and an oral tradition. The *Aenglish* didn't have written language until a thousand years later. The Jewish people belonged to different sects of Judaism with different beliefs and practices. These sects were the *Samaritans*, *Sadducees*, *Pharisees*, and the *Essenes*. The *Samaritans* believed the Pentateuch was the only Holy Scripture. At the center of the Hebrew religion was the Temple of David and an aristocratic hereditary priesthood, the *Sadducees*, who maintained the strictness of the temple tradition including animal sacrifices. The *Sadducees* only accepted worship in the temple as proper. They were the most conservative.

The *Pharisees*, a large and powerful more progressive sect accepted the written and the oral Hebrew tradition. The *Pharisees* did not believe that you had to worship in the temple or engage in animal sacrifices. Instead, they supported the rabbi and the synagogue as a place of worship and learning. The *Pharisees* believed in the immortality of the soul, angels, free will and a God that no human being could fully comprehend. The *Pharisees* were people who believed in living and worshipping separate from those who weren't Jewish, considering themselves "undefiled." They also hoped to bring other nations to their faith including the following of the *Torah*. There are many instances in the New Testament that record the *Pharisees'* strict support for the Jewish Law. There are many exchanges shown in the Bible between Jesus and the *Pharisees* who questioned Jesus about his activities that did not reflect Jewish Law.

The *Essenes* a much smaller sect, but very important to this story, existed from 200 B.C. to 70 A.D. These Jews were mostly male monastic groups who lived in closed, separate communities that held all things in common and sold their labors, generally agricultural, to support their communities. The *Essenes* had very strict hierarchy, rules, and daily schedules. They were the first to speak out against slavery and opposed the ownership of private property. The name *Essene* comes from a Greek term meaning "the holy ones" and an Aramaic term, "to heal." It may not be what they called themselves but ancient historians *Philo* and *Josephus* gave them that name. Although they lived in the cities they preferred the countryside or the "wilderness" to seek God. It took two years to become an *Essene* terminating with "election" or acceptance by the larger group. If you then became one of the "elect" you would be eligible to take your vows. The *Essenes* spent much of their time in prayer and studying the *Torah*. Each member was required to do daily manual labor. They observed a strict simple diet, offered no animal sacrifices, and spent much time communing with the angels.

The historian *Josephus* began the *Essene* training but did not finish the complete program so he did not become one of the elect. He revealed the *Essene* oath in his writings:

> To be pious to God, to practice justice towards men; never to injure anyone, whether of his own accord or under compulsion, always to hate the wicked and side with the just: ever to show faithfulness to all mankind and to be true to those in authority, for all power comes from God; never when in office to force his personal views of authority or to assume a special dress or luxury; to love truth and hate falsehood; to keep his hands pure of theft and his soul from unrighteous gain; not to have any secret from his brethren and never to betray one of theirs, even at the cost of his life; to pass on the traditions he himself had received; never to be a brigand; to safeguard the sacred books and to preserve, with care, the names of the angels that had been taught to him.

Josephus also wrote that *Essenes* were originally located in Egypt and had adopted doctrines of the *Pythagoreans* and the *Stoics*. *Josephus* reported that the *Essenes* worshipped facing the sun not the temple. The discovery after 1947 of parts of some 10,000 documents in the caves above the Dead Sea near the ruins of the *Essene Qumran* monastery has shed some new light on the early development of the Hebrew Bible, the Old Testament, and the *Essene* body of literature. Some caves appeared to be places of hermitage and others hidden depositories for important Hebrew documents possibly as the Romans advanced to destroy their community which happened around 70 A.D. These are the Dead Sea Scrolls and although they support the authenticity of Hebrew Biblical literature, there is no mention of Jesus by name or the term Christ in any of the documents found among them. They do show some of the roots of Jewish thought and practices during the time of Jesus' birth and afterward

The Essene Gospel Of Peace

In the 1920s, a young man named Edward Bordeaux Szekley took a vow of poverty and went to the Vatican where he spent a year researching St. Francis. Born in Transylvania, Szekley had studied in a Catholic high school run by a priest who was a personal friend of an archivist at the Vatican. This priest arranged for Szekley to continue his studies of original source material in Rome. Szekley, a young man with eyes wide open, found many other wonderful, ancient scrolls there that he believed the Nestorian priests had brought to the Vatican archives when running from the Mongols. Szekley eventually obtained his PhD from the University of Paris and was a philologist in *Sanskrit*, *Aramaic*, Greek and Latin. He spoke ten modern languages and was an undeniably gifted man. He published many small but important books in his lifetime beginning with the *Essene Gospel of Peace* in 1928. It was followed by three more volumes of interpreted scrolls he found in the Vatican written in *Aramaic* and others he found in the Royal Archives of the Habsburgs written in old Slavonic.

In Szekley's *The Essene Gospel of Peace Vol. 1.*, there is a chapter titled, *The Essene Gospel of Peace.* In this scripture translated by Szekley from *Aramaic*, Jesus speaks to an assemblage of varying "sick and maimed" people. They were asking him questions about life and he is answering their questions. Jesus speaks to them about purification of the body and mind, the ability to commune with the angels and experience the holy stream of life. Jesus speaks about the Holy Law and Scripture. Jesus also speaks of the Earthly Mother and the Heavenly Father who give us our body and spirit within whose laws we exist:

> And the many sick and maimed came to Jesus, asking him: "If you know all things, tell us, why do we suffer with these grievous plagues?
>
> And Jesus answered: "Happy are you, that you hunger for the truth, for I will satisfy you with the bread of wisdom. Happy are you that you knock, for I will open to you the door of life. Happy are you, that you would cast off the power of Satan, for I will lead you into the kingdom of our Mother's angels, where the power of Satan cannot enter."
>
> And they asked him in amazement: "Who is our Mother and which her angels? And where is her kingdom?"
>
> "Your mother is in you and you in her. She bore you: she gives you life. It was she who gave you your body, and to her shall you one day give it back again. Happy are you when you come to know her and her kingdom; if you receive your Mother's angels and if you do her laws. I tell you truly, he who does these things shall never see disease. For the power of our Mother is above all. And it destroys Satan and his kingdom, and has rule over all your bodies and all living things."
>
> And all those round him listened to his words with amazement, for his word was with power, and he taught quite otherwise than the priests and scribes.
>
> And though the sun was now set, they departed not to their homes. They sat round about Jesus and asked him: "Master, which are these laws of life? Rest with us

awhile longer and teach us. We would listen to your teaching that we may be healed and become righteous."

And Jesus himself sat down in their midst and said: "I tell you truly, none can be happy, except he who does the Law."

And the others answered: "We all do the laws of Moses, our lawgiver, even as they are written in the holy scriptures."

And Jesus answered: "Seek not the law in your scriptures, for the law is life, whereas the scripture is dead. I tell you truly, Moses received not his laws from God in writing, but through the living word. The law is living word of the living God to living prophets for living men. In everything that is life is the law written. You find it in the grass, in the tree, in the river, in the mountain, in the birds of heaven, in the fishes of the sea: but seek it chiefly in yourselves. For I tell you truly, all living things are nearer to God than the scripture which is without life. God so made life and all living things that they might by the everlasting word to teach the laws of the true God to man. God wrote not the laws in the pages of books, but in your heart and in your spirit. I tell you truly, that the scripture is the work of man, but life and all its hosts are the work of our God. Wherefore do you not listen to the words of God which are written in His works? And wherefore do you study the dead scriptures which are the works of the hands of men?"

"How may we read the laws of God elsewhere than in the scriptures? Where are they written? Read them to us from there where you see them, for we know nothing else but the scriptures which we have inherited from our forefathers. Tell us the laws of which you speak, that hearing them we may be healed and justified."

Jesus said: "You do not understand the words of life, because you are in death. Darkness darkens your eyes and your ears are stopped with darkness. For I tell you, it profits you not at all that you pore over dead scriptures if by your deeds you deny him who has given you the scriptures. I tell you truly, God and his laws are not in that which you do. They are not in gluttony and in wine-bibbing, neither in riotous living, not in lustfulness, nor in seeking after riches, nor yet in hatred of your enemies. For all these things are far from the true God and from his angels. But all these things come from the kingdom of darkness and the lord of all evils. All these things do you carry in yourselves; and so the word and the power of God enter not into you, because all manner of evil and all manner of abominations have their dwelling in your body and your spirit. If you will that the living God's word and his power may enter you, defile not your body and your spirit; for the body is the temple of the spirit, and the spirit is the temple of God. Purify, therefore, the temple, that the Lord of the temple may dwell therein and occupy a place that is worthy of him.

"Love one another, for God is love, and so shall his angels know that you walk in his paths."

Then Jesus rose. But all else remained sitting, for everyman felt the power of his words. And then the full moon appeared between the breaking clouds and folded Jesus in its brightness. And sparks flew upward from his hair, and he stood among them in the moonlight, as though he hovered in the air. And no man moved, neither was the voice of any heard. And no one knew how long a time had passed, for time stood still.

Then Jesus stretched out his hands to them and said: "Peace be with you." And so, departed, as a breath of wind sways the green trees.

These passages are from the first 25 pages of *The Essene Gospel of Peace*, translated by Szekely and published by the International Biogenic Society from Canada. They give you a flavor of a Jesus that speaks to the unhealthy world somewhat differently than the Jesus in the New Testament. Along with teaching peace, love and sharing, he is teaching about our "Earthly Mother" (Mother Earth) and ways to purify one's body that one may fully function in health to begin the path to a deeper understanding of what is going on in this universe. In the New Testament he taught "**our** Father who art in heaven." By stating **our** Heavenly Father, he is not separating himself from the rest of us as having a different origin or divine privilege. He is saying our body comes from our Mother Earth and it exists within her laws: Transgress them and see disease; learn them and live healthy. He speaks like a revolutionary telling his audience that if the scriptures are not words of life then they are nothing but dead words of dead men. He plainly states God's laws are found more truly in the grass or the leaves on the tree. He says to seek God's law, chiefly within our selves. Jesus ended his discourse with these words about peace:

> Till now you were at war with your Father, with your Mother, and with your Brothers. And you have served Satan. From today live at peace with your Heavenly Father, and with your Earthly Mother, and with your Brothers, the Sons of Men. And fight only against Satan, lest he rob you of your peace. I give the peace of your Earthly Mother, to your body, and the peace of your Heavenly Father to your spirit. And let the peace of both reign among the Sons of Men.
>
> Come to me, all that are weary and that suffer in strife and affliction! For my peace will strengthen you and comfort you. For my peace is exceedingly full of joy. Wherefore do I always greet you after this manner: "Peace be with you!" Do you always, therefore, so greet one another, that upon your body may descend the peace of the Earthly Mother, and upon your spirit the peace of

the Heavenly Father. And then you will find peace among yourselves, for the kingdom of God is within you. And now return to your Brothers with whom hither to you were at war, and give your peace to them also. For happy are they that strive for peace, for they will find the peace of God. Go, and sin no more. And give to every one your peace, even as I have given mine unto you. For my peace is of God. Peace be with you.

The portion of the *Essene* Gospel ended with this commentary:

And he left them.

And his peace descended upon them; And in their heart the angel of love, in their head the wisdom of law, and in their hands the power of rebirth, they went forth among the Sons of Men, to bring the light of peace to those that warred in darkness.

And they parted, wishing one to another.

PEACE BE WITH YOU.

These are very powerful and wonderful words from Jesus who came back to the land of his people after being gone for many years on his own path of development. He returned to provide healing through his teachings and by his example. The New Testament does not speak of Jesus' life from his early teens to around his 30th year when he returns to the Hebrew people. Jesus was obviously gone a long distance for a long time because the people and the priests did not know him when he returned. If you look at maps of the ancient Silk Road you will see that it connected Jerusalem with China by crossing India on the north side of the Himalayas. There are many people in India who believe Jesus and possibly his mother traveled to these sacred mountains and studied with the *Yogis* and *Lamas* there.

Evidence That Jesus Traveled To India And Tibet

Paramahansa Yogananda, a Hindu yogi born in India in 1893, arrived in America in 1920 to represent a Hindu perspective of India as a delegate to the International Congress of Religious Liberals in Boston, Massachusetts. *Yogananda* had been studying with a guru for many years in his homeland, and during his studies he had traveled to many sacred sites and met many *yogis* and *gurus* each with their own saintly gifts. He was raised by a religious father within the mystic stream of holiness of an ancient religious tradition. *Yogananda* died in 1952 after founding, in this country, the Self Realization Fellowship. He authored many books. His most famous work is, *Autobiography of a Yogi*. In his book, *The Second Coming of Christ—the Resurrection of the Christ Within You,* he wrote about Jesus' travels to India and Tibet:

> Remarkable accounts, however, do exist, not in the land of Jesus' birth but farther east where he spent most of the unaccounted-for years. Hidden away in a Tibetan monastery priceless records lie. They speak of a Saint Issa from Israel "in whom was manifest the soul of the universe"; who from the age of fourteen to twenty-eight was in India and regions of the Himalayas among saints, monks, and pundits; who preached his message throughout that area and then returned to teach in his native land, where he was treated vilely, condemned, and put to death.

Yogananda wrote about the controversial Russian traveler Nicholas Notovitch who traveled around India in the late 1800s. There he heard the stories locals near *Kashmir* told about the visit of the Saint. Notovitch also heard about ancient manuscripts located in a Tibetan monastery. He traveled to the *Himis* monastery in *Ladakh*. On his first trip, the monks would not show him nor acknowledge the manuscripts he sought. On the trip home while crossing a mountain passage by horseback, he broke his leg. He was taken back to the monastery for refuge and during this visit he was shown the manuscripts of his interest. These ancient manuscripts were interpreted to him from Tibetan into French. From his notes he published the book, *The Unknown Life of Jesus* in 1894. Many people challenged Notovitch's character and writings.

Yogananda told of two other reputable people who traveled to the region and saw and heard the same stories:

> In 1922, *Swami Abhedananda*, a direct disciple of *Ramakrishna Paramahansa*, visited the *Himi* Monastery, and confirmed all the salient details about Issa published in Notovitch's book.
>
> Nicholas Roerich, in an expedition to India and Tibet in the mid-1920s, saw and copied verses from ancient manuscripts that were the same, or at least the same content, as those published by Notovich. He was also deeply impressed by the oral traditions of the area: "In Srinagar we first encountered the curious legend of the visit of Christ to this place. Afterwards we saw how widely spread in India, in Ladak and in Central Asia, was the legend of the visit of Christ to these parts during his long absence, quoted in the Gospel."

These stories relate how Jesus came of age at 13 and would have had an arranged marriage according to the tradition of his people. To avoid this, he secretly joined a caravan headed for the Orient and the seat of ancient spirituality, India. *Yogananda* related the story:

The name by which Jesus is identified in the Tibetan manuscripts is *Isa* ("Lord"), rendered by Notovitch as *Issa*. *Isa* (*Isha*), or its extension *Ishvara*, defines God as the Supreme Lord or Creator immanent in as well as transcendent of His creation. This is the true character of the Christ/Krishna, and other God-united souls who possess oneness with the Lord's omnipresence. It is my conviction that the title *Isa* was given at birth to Jesus by the Wise Men from India who came to honor his advent on earth. In the New Testament, Jesus' disciples commonly refer to him as "Lord."

The ancient history relates that Jesus became learned in all the *Vedas* and *shastras*. But he took issue with some precepts of the Brahminic orthodoxy. He openly denounced their practices of caste bigotry; many of the priestly rituals, and the emphasis on the worship of many gods in idolic form rather than sole reverence for the one Supreme Spirit, the pure monotheistic essence of Hinduism which had become obscured by outer ritualistic concepts.

Distancing himself from these disputes, Jesus left Puri. He spent the next six years with the *Sakya* Buddhist sect in the Himalayan mountainous regions of Nepal and Tibet. This Buddhist sect was monotheistic, having separated itself from the distorted Hinduism that prevailed during the dark age of Kali Yuga.

All this is not to say that Jesus learned everything he taught from his spiritual mentors and associated in India and surrounding regions. Avatars come with their own endowment of wisdom. Jesus' store of divine realization was merely awakened and molded to fit his unique mission by his sojourn among the Hindu pundits, Buddhist monks, and particularly the great masters of yoga from whom he received initiation in the esoteric science of God-union through meditation. From the knowledge he had gleaned, and from the wisdom brought forth from his soul in deep meditation, he distilled for the masses simple parables of the ideal principles by which to govern one's life in the sight of God. But to those disciples who were ready to receive it, he taught deeper mysteries, as evidenced in the New Testament book of Revelation of St. John, the symbology of which accords exactly with the yoga science of God-realization.

Professor James Deardorff of Oregon State University wrote a scholarly study of Notovich's work and the documents criticizing it, from which he published a paper and a book on the *Lost Years of Jesus*. Deardorff believed Notovich's critics did not use scholarly arguments. He found the similarity of *Swami Abhedananda's* interpreted verses and Notovich's work to be sound. *Abhedananda* published a book about his travels with the *Issa* verses. *Abhedananda's* book was translated into English in 1987. Deardorff described a portion of the book:

> The Swami ordered and numbered his set of *Isa* verses after the manner of Notovich's set; however, the set he presented contained far fewer verses than the 244 within Notovich's set, which is consistent with *Abhedananda* mentioning that his set was derived from just one book at the monastery, while Notovich had mentioned a second book or manuscript being involved also. In addition, however, *Abhedananda* omitted publication of many verses, apparently because they contain material that could be deemed offensive to different braches of Hinduism. Comparison of those verses that are common to the two sets of *Isa* text indicates little difference in substance but very appreciable differences in sentence structure and detail, as is to be expected from different translators and languages of translation having been involved.

Deardorff also commented on an Issa tradition in Afghanistan:

> The traditions are known also in northwestern Afghanistan, centered at heart, by some thousand devotees of *Isa*, son of *Maryam*, who live within several scattered villages. This has been brought out by O.M. Burke who personally interviewed their spiritual leader, *Abba Yahiyya* (Father John), while researching Sufism in this area of the globe. However, these traditions are not particulary well known outside of their local areas, and there is no indication that Notovich knew before coming upon word of the existence of a manuscript or two at *Himis* to the effect that Jesus had been there in his travels during his youth.

In my studies I find no significant contradiction between the teaching of Jesus, the Eastern spiritual teachings represented by *Parahamansa Yogananda*, and Buddhist teachings about how to live our lives with our fellow human beings. I see them as coming from the same source, interaction with the One Universal essence. These great teachers show human beings how to be truly happy, healthy, joyful and peaceful while on Earth. The Bible records many truths as it presents the words of Jesus. It does not however present the complete story of Jesus' life and his teachings. The Bible is, as we have discussed earlier, a selected assemblage of texts that evolved from the Nicean Council of 325 A.D. The Bible presents only the Alexandrian side of the story and the creed developed there. It does not present the Arian or the *Gnostic* or other beliefs that co-existed before the council. Today, in the Information Age we are able to find more of the pieces of the ancient puzzle that survived because they were hidden away.

In the New Testament, Jesus clearly taught the purification of the heart so that natural love could manifest and flow through the heart. He taught us not to get caught up in the material world of lust and treasure. As the story is related, "Satan" showed him the empires of the world and told him that all of this could be his if he would deny Love and seek control of Empire.

Sanskrit Sutras Teaching The Development of Love

Around 1900, *Yogananda's* teacher in India, *Swami Sri Yukteswar* wrote a small book, at the request of an Indian saint, *Babaji*, to show the similarity of Jesus' teachings and the ancient Indian *Sanskrit Sutras* that are studied in India. The task was proposed by *Babaji* and accepted by *Sri Yukteswar* when they met in 1894 at a spiritual festival in *Allahabad*, India. Their meeting produced the ideas for the book *The Holy Science*. *Sri Yukteswar* stated:

> The purpose of this book is to show as clearly as possible that there is an essential unity in all religions; that there is no difference in the truths inculcated by the various faiths; that there is but one method by which the world, both external and internal, has evolved; and that there is but one Goal admitted by all scriptures. But this basic truth is one not easily comprehended. The discord existing between the different religions, and the ignorance of men, make it almost impossible to lift the veil and have a look at this grand verity. The creeds foster hostility and dissension; ignorance widens the gulf that separates one creed from another.

He interprets a *Sanskrit Sutra* and then relates it to a Bible passage. I have chosen a couple important examples from his book:

SUTRAS 5, 6

Aum is heard through cultivation of *Sraddha* (heart's natural love), V*irya* (moral courage), *Smriti* (memory of one's divinity), and *Samadhi* (true concentration).

Sraddha is intensification of the heart's natural love. The virtue of Love. The heart's natural love is the principal requisite to attain holy life. When this love, the heavenly gift of Nature, appears in the heart, it removes all causes of excitation from the system and cools down to a perfectly normal state; and invigorating the vital powers, expels all foreign matters—the germs of diseases—by natural ways (perspiration and so forth). It thereby makes man perfectly healthy in body and mind, and enables him to understand properly the guidance of Nature.

When this love becomes developed in man it makes him able to understand the real position of his own Self as well as of others surrounding him.

With the help of this developed love, man, becomes fortunate in gaining the Godlike company of the divine personages and is saved forever. Without this love, man cannot live in the natural way, neither can he keep company with the fit person for his own welfare; he becomes often excited by the foreign matters taken into his system through mistakes in understanding the guidance of Nature, and in consequence he suffers in body and mind. He can never find peace whatever, and his life becomes a burden. Hence the culture of this love, the heavenly gift, is the principle requisite for the attainment of holy salvation; it is impossible for man to advance a step toward the same without it. See Revelation 2:2–4

SUTRAS 12–18

Hence bondage disappears.

The eight bondages or snares are hatred, shame, fear, grief, condemnation, race prejudice, pride of family, and smugness.

(Removal of the eight bondages) leads to magnanimity of heart.

The eight meannesses of the heart. Firmness of moral courage, when attained, removes all the obstacles in the way of salvation. These obstacles are of eight sorts—hatred, shame, fear, grief, condemnation, race prejudice, pride of pedigree, and a narrow sense of respectability—which eight are the meannesses of the human heart.

SUTRA 24

In the dark state of heart, man harbors misconceptions (about everything). This state is a result of *Avidya*, Ignorance, and produces a *Sudra* (a man of the lowest caste). He can grasp only ideas of the physical world. This state of mind is prevalent in Kali Yuga, the Dark Age of a cycle.

The dark heart. In the dark state of the heart man misconceives; he thinks that this gross material portion of the creation is the only real substance in existence, and that there is nothing besides. However, this is contrary to the truth, as has been explained before, and is nothing but the effect of Ignorance, *Avidya*.

CONCLUSION

"Love rules the court, the camp, the grove,
The men below and saints above;
For love is heaven and heaven is love,"

The poet quoted in the stanza above beautifully described the power of love. It has been clearly demonstrated in the foregoing pages that "Love is God," not merely as the noblest sentiment of a poet but as an aphorism of eternal truth. To whatever religious creed a man may belong and whatever may be his position in society, if he properly cultivates this ruling principle naturally implanted in his heart, he is sure to be on the right path for salvation to save himself from wandering in this creation of Darkness, *Maya*.

It has been shown in the foregoing pages how love may be cultivated, how by its culture it attains development, and when developed, through this means only, how man may find his Spiritual Preceptor, through whose favor he again becomes baptized in the holy stream, and sacrifices his Self before the altar of God, becoming unified with the Eternal Father forever and ever.

I have chosen these *Sutras* and their interpretations from *Sri Yukteswar's* work as important core concepts of the development of love in our hearts and the power of love in our life. It is the same love that Jesus taught us to follow and keep in our hearts. It is the opposite of being a warrior or Viking who would kill his fellow man for personal gain or whatever reason given by his leaders. If you love your neighbor and your enemy, you will not hoard and withhold what your neighbor needs, especially food, medicine, and emotional support. Human beings have many potential behavior patterns. In general we want to do what is right and we follow the instruction of credible figures or role models we knit into our character in our young lives. Lets start a new day in a new way and follow these great teachers' examples of love and service to our fellow man, not hoarding, competition, and selfishness.

Current mainline Christianity teaches that we live on this Earth one time but our souls are eternal. These souls are judged, according to how they lived, and at the end of this life our eternal fate is determined. Most Christians subscribe to the belief that God created but one son, Jesus. He then killed his one son in a torturous death so that he could cleanse the sins of all (believers) mankind.

Eastern religion teaches each human being is an eternal soul on a path of development through the learning of many lifetimes. Once the soul has completed learning it returns to God to incarnate not again on this Earth. It also teaches that all of the Universe is created through Gods thought however man has freewill choice to act as he or she chooses while incarnate and so is also personally responsible for those thoughts and actions.

It is clear that Jesus was an expression of the living God to the living men of his time. He made no written record to be left for the ages. *What Jesus was or is, each person can decide but one thing is very clear, Jesus taught us to love and to share, not to kill and hoard.*

9

Moving Towards Our Higher Human Potential In One Universe

Our culture is operating on many of the assumptions that were developed in a time when the perspective on the universe was much smaller for the Anglo-Saxons and the Romans. At that time, the Earth was thought to be the center of the universe and everything revolved around it. A tribal area was the center of everything and all people and places outside of that area were thought of as different. When Anglo-Saxons began to manipulate iron, they began to feel very powerful over their surroundings and over the other living things. Using iron, fasteners were made to hold together the wooden dragon ships that were long and flexible with shallow drafts that could cross oceans and sneak up close for the surprise raid. They used iron to make effective weapons, tools, and shields.

Anglo-Saxons recognized some males among their tribesmen who had the *divine privilege* of being fathered by their god/creator of the earth, *Woden*. That belief made those males royalty. Having these divinely sired men made the tribe very special, in their own minds. It was evidence that God was on their side. These warrior kings from these "divinely sired" bloodlines eventually became the English royalty. The combination of cultural ethnocentric assumptions of divine privilege, Viking warrior mentality, and the highly developed craftsmanship of iron weapons allowed the Anglo-Saxons to dominate and displace other races and cultures. This philosophy of domination is the foundation of our racial and cultural superiority viewpoint that we see even today through our own acts of military domination and invasion of other countries. This sort of cultural and racial primacy existed as the norm in northern Germany 1600 years ago, and it has afforded us our comfortable lifestyle today. These same assumptions are leading to violence and destruction on a much larger scale on Earth in the race for hoarded wealth and military domination. Philosophies of superiority and competitive living need to be reexamined and left behind.

Rome had a similar perspective regarding their culture and their emperors. In their cosmology, the Romans had many gods all interacting in the god world or dimension and roamed the human world. The Romans had emperors who were gods, and gods who sired children among human beings. The Roman emperors were thought to be gods or sent by god to rule. The Roman Emperor Constantine, who allied himself with Christianity and developed the Holy Roman Church, exemplified this divine privilege. Constantine grew up with the idea of divine privilege, and believed in this same privilege until the end of his life. Emperors and kings exist through the blessings of the cultural assumption of divine privilege. These are the roots of **divine privilege** still operating in the world today.

The religious dogma of Christianity we know today was developed through the power of the Roman Empire supporting the idea of divine privilege. The Roman Church story of Jesus related that he was sired from a male god and a human woman. This story is part of what separates him from the body of humanity, and granted Jesus the status of being the only true Son of God. Jesus demonstrated this divinity according to the Roman Church story by performing miracles and resurrecting from the dead. This same orthodox authority told ordinary human beings they were born as sinners because they inherited the "original" sin of Adam and Eve. According to this orthodox story, ordinary human beings do not have the same divine inheritance from the creator of the universe. This story makes humanity subservient to kings and priests. It maintains both orders. The system has worked well to maintain the order for kings, emperors and the priesthood.

Most of us in today's world if presented with a story of a god fathering a child would not accept the story or the teller of the tale. Today, the story doesn't fit into our modern scientific cosmology. In general, it is not a story that is given to adults to process; it is a story given to children by adults. Children accept the story and knit it into their cosmology. I am not saying that Jesus was not very special or to be held in any less esteem but there is more to the story. Jesus was showing us the way to live and made great sacrifice through his nonviolent, nonresistance to evil.

I believe that Jesus came of age studying the Jewish Law and then began his travels to further develop and learn more. He learned the ancient art and science of meditation with the

Yoga masters in India and the Buddhist monks of Tibet, masters of the practices. He was able to master practices that helped him develop to his full human and divine potential to be in full communion with the creative intelligence saturating the universe. He demonstrated the power of a pure heart and a developed human being to interact with the creative intelligent force that is behind All matter in the One Universe.

In the face of new scientific evidence and hidden ancient secrets that I will briefly relate in this chapter, I hope that you will openly consider the possibility that Jesus the Christ was a highly developed human being showing us the highest human potentials. If one follows the path Jesus showed us, then one must work hard to cleanse one's body, thoughts, and actions to become a loving, peaceful, sharing human being. This is a hard road of change in a world where we are sold such a different way.

One Universe Under Intelligence

Our home, the Earth, is a planet orbiting a star that is one star among over 100 trillion within our home galaxy. Our galaxy is one of over 100 trillion other galaxies showing trillions of stars in each of those within the visible universe. The visible end of the universe is not in sight. The currently known universe is huge beyond comprehension. This massive universe is probably all made of the same 100 or so types of natural elements arranged in many different configurations that are the common building blocks of the entire visible universe. The same laws of physics are operating throughout. I think that the universe is all One and created from the same source or sources.

Our planet probably contains a unique mixture of materials, and its position in relation to the star it orbits may also be uncommon but it is not totally unique as the only one in creation. The forces unfolding here on Earth are a part of those throughout the larger universe.

We can see intelligence as a property of every living cell observable with the microscope. I see intelligence born in all creatures, including plants and insects as they fulfill their roles within the cycles of the seasons in our world. Where there is life there is intelligence. Knowing that this planet is not an isolated, separate place, it appears that life and intelligence are properties of this universe. From the bare stone, wherever the conditions are right, single cell life begins to work together to build environments for larger creatures, as James Dillet Freeman said, "the mud that would not lie still." The planet and all the living creatures that live upon it are part of something larger than our ability to comprehend.

Our bodies are fabulous constructions that develop along a plan from two single cells (ova and sperm). The design of our bodies is amazingly complex, and works very well. How does nature come up with such beautiful, complicated and functioning designs? As a craftsman/designer, I see that it takes applied intelligence for designs to work. Nothing put together from random accident will work right, and it will not be beautiful as the many living creations on our world. It is an easy deduction for me to see that intelligence is at work here in the many beautiful complicated manifestations of life working so well on Earth. This intelligence is a force as large as the universe not just an isolated occurrence on this planet, separate from the rest.

Science is a wonderful tool for developing an understanding of some of the workings of this infinitely complicated world and the larger universe. Science can alleviate suffering or it can cause great suffering depending upon how it is used. However, science is limited in its scope and possibility by its current mechanical view of the universe and its dependence upon human cognitive and physical ability. Human beings can only see (with their eyeballs) in this vast universe certain wavelengths of light, hear certain wavelengths of sound, and perceive thoughts of limited complexity and complication with their brains and physical senses. In this vast universe as we look out and in, humans and the mechanical technologies they can produce are the limiting factor to science. If human minds cannot conceive the equation, science cannot prove its truth.

The Hubble Finds Dark Energy And Dark Matter

Our mechanical technology has been dramatically improving in recent years with the advent of computerized machinery. It has allowed us to see greater spectrums of what exists on the macro and micro scale. The Hubble telescope and its discoveries are an example of this. By getting the Hubble telescope outside the Earth's atmosphere we have been able to see deeper and clearer into the universe. Many amazing things have been discovered. The Hubble telescope has photographed new views of our universe, including new discoveries confirming what has been termed *dark energy*. The phenomenon is called dark energy because it is a force that appears to be adding energy to the motion of the universe, however, dark energy does not give off light or radiation in spectrums we can see or detect, so it is called dark. Scientists observing the light of an exploding supernova as it moved across the universe discovered dark energy. The Hubble detects these brief, great flashes of light that can be seen at great distances. These flashes remind the astronomers of popping corn: the brief poof of the kernel as it explodes. By watching this flash of light come across the universe, astronomers and mathematicians learned that the universe is expanding at an accelerating rate.

If the Big Bang hypothesis is correct and energy of an expanding universe came in the beginning with one huge cosmic bang, that energy should be slowing down as the force of gravity acts on the matter. Astronomer Dr. Adam Riese, of the Space Telescope Science Institute, headquarters of Hubble stated on the National Public Radio program, Earth and Sky:

> In 1998, or a few years predating that, our team had made observations of the expansion rate of the universe. And at that time, our expectation, and in fact, for the whole scientific community's expectation of that was that we would see the expansion rate of the universe gradually slowing down after the Big Bang as a result of all the self attraction of all the material in the universe. And, what we actually saw was quite shocking and surprising. We actually saw that the expansion rate of the universe was getting faster and faster all the time. And it was very hard to understand why that was, but at that time we and the scientific community came to the strange conclusion that the universe appears to be filled with this dark energy material that acts repulsively, and causes the universe to speed up all the time. This is not completely unprecedented in thought or deed. Einstein had suggested this as just a theoretical possibility back in the 1920's . . . And we're still struggling to understand what this dark energy is, what its nature is, what kind of physics causes it, and what it means for the ultimate fate

of the universe. So we continue today to make observations on the dark energy. In my work I use the Hubble telescope to do this work . . . We hope to pinpoint what this dark energy is.

I guess the biggest surprise to me is that this result continues to hold up. There have been a number of different cosmological experiments that have nothing to do with the technique that we've used, so not using supernovae—looking at the heat left over from the Big Bang, looking at distant clusters of galaxies and differences in properties that you can measure of those observables have come to the exact same conclusions, that the universe is filled with dark energy.

So, we're trying to measure these two properties of the dark energy, its strength and its permanence. And right now, we have only the beginnings of very weak knowledge about either of those properties. But, from what we've seen, it's permanence indicates that it may be completely permanent, it may never have changed at all, but what we can rule out from the data is that it certainly hasn't changed very much over the last few billion years. Ultimately, if we want to know what the fate of the universe is, we have to know where the dark energy is taking the universe. Literally, at this juncture, dark energy is sort of in charge in terms of the dynamic of the universe.

Scientists have also developed the term of *dark matter* because of other properties they see invisibly at work in the outer space of the universe. It has been observed that something invisible appears to be holding together spinning galaxies, keeping them from flying apart in their spinning. The visible universe appears to be embedded in this dark matter. *Dark matter* is estimated to have greater mass than the visible universe. Here we have major forces in the universe that scientists cannot see but instead deduce their presence by observing their action upon visible matter and light. Scientists also deduce that the visible universe comes from this invisible material they call dark matter.

Over a hundred years ago Hindu and Buddhist holy men wrote of this force moving the galaxy and stated that space was full of a finer particle of matter than the atom. They also wrote that this finer particle has the property of intelligence. How could they have such knowledge? What was the origin of their discovery?

India has had a developed system of esoteric spiritual knowledge for over 4000 years. The *Vedas* are ancient written teachings still studied today. These are the written lessons of an accumulation of many teachers. In India, devotees seeking spiritual development find *gurus* and *yogis* to show them the path to human higher development. Their spirituality is rooted in these *Vedas* and the *Bhagavad Gita*. Buddhism is also rooted in the same tradition of this area. *Guatama Buddha* was born an Indian *Brahman* raised in the *Vedic* tradition before he took his teachings to the larger Oriental world. There is evidence that Jesus of Nazareth also traveled and studied these same teachings, bringing the concept "God is love" back to the West.

In the late 1800s during the British occupation of India, a few of the English people became interested in the esoteric facets of Hinduism and Tibetan Buddhism. Some of the English occupiers saw and heard about miraculous acts of men addressed by the local people as *Yogi*. These individuals appeared to have conscious control over involuntary systems of their body among other things. The *yogis* had renounced worldly possessions similar to some Christian monks and lived as teachers or wondering healers.

Mahatmas And Yogi's Perspective

In England and the United States during the late 1800s, the stories of miraculous phenomena led to the development of different movements seeking knowledge in the unseen dimensions of human life. One of these spiritual movements exists today. Helena Blavotsky, a very controversial figure, founded the Theosophical Society. Blavotsky a very spiritually intuitive woman was born a Russian noblewoman into the man's world of the 1800s. She grew up in the Russian privileged class and traveled the world dressed as a man for freedom of travel. Her travels led her to Tibet, among other places, where she studied with Buddhist masters. What she brought to the Western world provided the Theosophical Society and Theosophical Press with a large body of literature that is still being published in Pasadena, California. The books dwell on the Buddhist cosmology of the universe and the path of compassion for humanity's development of its higher nature.

One very interesting book published by the Theosophical Press is *The Mahatma Letters*. The book is an accumulation of letters written by a couple of Buddhist *Mahatmas* (who were Helena Blavotsky's teachers) to an editor of an English newspaper in India during the late 1800s. These letters were a part of a long exchange between A.P. Sinnet the editor of *The Pioneer* and these *Mahatmas*. Sinnet was a member of the Theosophical Society seeking ancient truth and he struggled to fit these beliefs into his cosmology. The *Mahatmas* were seeking to explain the functioning of the universe, from their perspectives in a language (English) that did not and does not have words for much of what they were trying to explain. The letters themselves are in the British Museum. The letters are sometimes long and wordy with dry humor of the times. Here is an excerpt about the movement of our galaxy and the nature of "space."

> The whole of our system is imperceptibly shifting its position in space. The relative distance between planets remaining ever the same, and being in no wise affected by the displacement of the whole system; and the distance between the latter and the stars and other suns being so incommensurable as to produce but little perceptible change for centuries and millenniums to come— no astronomer will perceive it *telescopically*, until Jupiter and some other planets, whose little luminous points hide now from our sight millions upon millions of stars (all but some 5000 or 6000)—will suddenly let us have a peep at a few of the *Raja-Suns* they are now hiding.
>
> The only great truth uttered by Siemens is that interstellar space is filled with highly attenuated matter, such as may be put in air vacuum tubes, and which stretches from planet to planet and from star to star. (Simla October 1882 K.H.)

Here is another excerpt from the *Mahatmas* on the intelligent force behind the material manifestation of the visible universe:

> Did it ever strike you—and now from the standpoint of your Western science and the suggestion of your own Ego which has already sized up the essentials of every truth, prepare to deride the erroneous idea—did you ever suspect that Universal, like finite, human mind might have two attributes or a dual power—one voluntary and conscious, and the other the involuntary and unconscious or mechanical power . . . Contrary in that to the finite, the "infinite mind," which we name so but for agreement sake, for we call it the infinite FORCE . . . It is the pecu-

liar faculty of the involuntary power of the infinite mind to be eternally evolving subjective matter into objective atoms or cosmic matter to be later developed into form.

Paramahansa Yogananda in several of his writings spoke of what he calls lifetrons, the smaller than atomic particles that are intelligent which make up our astral body and the whole astral world, a universe full of this material.

Sri Yukteswar used the word *prana*, I have translated it as lifetrons. The Hindu scriptures refer not only to the *anu*, "atom", and to the *paramanu*, "beyond the atom," but also to *prana*, "creative lifetronic force." Atoms and electrons are blind forces; *prana* is inherently intelligent. (Autobiography)

Sparks of intelligent, finer-than-atomic energy that constitute life, collectively referred to in Hindu scriptural treatises as *prana*, which Paramansha Yogananda has translated as "lifetrons." In essence, condensed thoughts of God; substance of the astral world (*q.v.*) and life principle of the physical cosmos. In the physical world, there are two kinds of *prana*: (1) the cosmic vibratory energy that is omnipresent in the universe, structuring and sustaining all things; (2) the specific *prana* or energy that pervades and sustains each human body through five currents or functions. (*Glossary of The Second Coming of the Christ Within You*)

Human Interaction With The Zero Point Energy Field

On the microscopic level, scientists are currently publishing many findings that are challenging the early scientific theory models of what human beings are, what matter is, and how these things interrelate. The study of quantum physics has begun opening the doors to new understandings of what matter at the atomic and subatomic level is as a part of what they call the Zero Point Field. This Zero Point Field long ignored by scientists is viewed by some as an electrical/magnetic field that interconnects all matter and the source of energy for all spinning electrons. It is believed that atomic particles move in and out of being in this field. It is also believed that information is stored in this field and that our brains are receivers of this information. As more is discovered about this relationship between living beings and this electro/magnetic field we may begin to redefine human beings and all living things away from the notion of simple mechanical/chemical reactions of chance. Writer Lynn McTaggart has produced an amazing book *The Field: The Quest for the Secret Force in the Universe,* in which she summarizes much of this research for lay people. She stated:

> What they have discovered is nothing less than astonishing. At our most elemental, we are not a chemical reaction, but an energetic charge. Human beings and all living things are a coalescence of energy in a field of energy connected to every other thing in the world. This pulsating energy field is the central engine of our being and *our consciousness*, the alpha and omega of our existence . . . .
>
> As the pioneers of quantum physics peered into the very heart of matter, they were astounded by what they saw. The tiniest bits of matter weren't even matter, as we know it, not even a set *something* . . .
>
> If the Zero Point Field were included in our conception of the most fundamental nature of matter, they realized, the very underpinning of our universe was a heaving sea of energy—*one* vast quantum field. If this

were true, everything would be connected to everything else like some invisible web.

They also discovered that we were made of the same basic material. On our most fundamental level, living beings, were packets of quantum energy constantly exchanging information with this inexhaustible energy sea. Living things emitted a weak radiation, and this was the most crucial aspect of biological processes. Thinking, feeling—every higher cognitive function—had to do with quantum information pulsing simultaneously through our brains and body. Human perception occurred because of interactions between the subatomic particles of our brains and the quantum energy sea. We literally resonated with our world.

A field is a matrix or medium which connects two or more points in space, usually via a force, like gravity or electromagnetism.

In the quantum world, quantum fields are not mediated by forces but by exchange of energy, which is constantly redistributed in a dynamic pattern. This constant exchange is an intrinsic property of particles, so that even 'real' particles are nothing more than a little knot of energy which briefly emerges and disappears back into the underlying field.

This sort of emission and reabsorbtion of virtual particles occurs not only among photons and electrons, but with all the quantum particles in the universe. Every exchange of the virtual particle radiates energy.

Electrons get their energy to keep going without slowing down because they are refueling by tapping into these fluctuations of empty space.

One of the most important aspects of waves is that they are *encoders and carriers of information.*

Her book is the summary of in-depth scientific research completed at Stanford, Princeton, and international universities. I had to read it twice to be able to summarize here. Her points are very important to a new conception of human beings, consciousness, the brain, and the universe. In studying where memories were stored it was discovered that there is no specific place in the brain but that the brain seems to be retrieving information stored in the Zero Point Field. In studying how vision forms 3-dimensional models in the brain it has been discovered that we are perceiving holographic information from the Field and our brain is reconstructing this information rather than reflecting a simple light and mirror model of earlier science. Our brains are constantly interacting with this Zero Point Field.

Science Shows That Prayer Helps Healing

These findings lead to studies of our human ability to remotely influence many things with our intentions since the workings of our minds are not contained within the chemicals of our head. Important to this story are the findings that ordinary human beings have the ability to remotely influence healing in other people, plant growth, bacterial activity, small mammal behavior and electrical Random Event Generators. In several studies on the effect of prayer it has been proven that ordinary people can help people with HIV and heart conditions heal and be happier and healthier. These studies were done with good protocol. The subjects did not know they were part of any study and the healers never entered the building where the sick patients were. Dr. Randolph Byrd conducted such a study in 1988 with 400 subjects in a coronary care unit. The results are published in the *Southern Medical Journal,* 1988, 81(7): 826–9. McTaggart summarized such a study like this:

All patients had been evaluated, and there was no statistical difference in their condition before treatment. However, after treatment, those who'd been prayed for had significantly less severe symptoms and fewer instances of pneumonia and also required less assistance on a ventilator and fewer antibiotics than patients who hadn't been prayed for.

Dr. Elisabeth Targ and psychologist Fred Sicher have conducted at least two studies on the effects of prayer on HIV ill patients. Both studies were very tightly designed and run. Both studies significantly proved that prayer affects healing positively. One big difference between Byrd's findings and Targ's studies was the prayer workers for Byrd were Christians and Targ's healers were of many different religious faiths. It does not seem to matter what or to whom you pray, to help but rather your intention to help seems to be of the greatest importance. Sicher and Targ's findings are published in the *Western Journal of Medicine*, 1998,168(6): 356–63.

Human Beings Can Affect the Operation Of Electrical Equipment With Intentions

At Princeton and Stanford they built electrical devices that produced random events such as lights that blinked red or green with a 50/50 chance of repeating one way or the other. The little lights blinked randomly but on average half the time red and half the time green. These were very fine devices working at the atomic level to produce random events. Through many studies of many different kinds, these researchers found that ordinary human beings could with their thoughts or intentions effect the operation of the Random

Event Generators (REG) to a significant degree. Some people had a statistically stronger effect upon these machines than other people. They found that bonded couples could produce a stronger effect on the REG machines than an individual when they willed it together. Researchers found that groups of people not even focusing on the REG machines but feeling or concentrating together on some other emotional event could be registered upon the machines. They placed these machines at several different places around the world and at the moment in time when the O.J. Simpson verdict was handed down all the machines registered deviation.

Our consciousness functions in our brains but it appears our intentions are not limited to affecting only our own bodies. Some human beings have more developed natural abilities to heal others and some can even remotely influence events. The ability to heal and interact with the Zero Point Field may be an ability that can be further developed through training or other processes of the living experience. Our universe is saturated with intelligence and the intelligence of human beings is but a small part of the Universal intelligence. Human beings can and do interact with the greater Universal intelligence in many ways. We must get our bodies, hearts, and minds in harmony to develop our abilities to their highest potential to interact with the Universal intelligence. As a first step we must purify our bodies by eating and drinking what is most healthy for us. We need to meditate regularly to clear our minds, develop that natural love in our hearts with good thoughts, speak good words when possible, and do good works.

Most of us in the Western world are totally ignorant of the potential for human development in this direction. This kind of development is not a path of cognitive knowledge like the process one follows to obtain a PhD. This path of compassion is opposite of acquiring the knowledge of how to amass resources of power and money. The killing of our fellow human beings is also contrary to this path. It is a spiritual path. It is developing our hearts and minds together in a way that leads to a direct experience of the higher and finer powers that exist in the universe and within our selves. This is the path of human development taught by the Hindu *Yogis*, Buddhist *Mahatmas*, and originally by Jesus the Christ. In our current world where our culture is loaded with violence, lust, greed, noise, and where so many people eat and drink unhealthy things, it will not be easy to make a change. This spiritual/natural way of living is the path of loving, sharing, and caring for our world and those beings manifesting in it.

Building The Common Spiritual Link Between All Souls

It is an important time, right now, for us to begin to make changes everyday. My intuition and my heart have been leading the quest of my mind to find answers in the ancient hidden truths that support what my intuition knows to be true. All human beings are created equal by the same force in a huge universe. No race or individual is created with specially granted divine privilege or loved by the creator more than any of his/her other children. We each need to come to the self-realization that we are each a child of the One Universe filled with the creative intelligent force of creation commonly called God. We each have a divine inheritance and we each are worthy. We are not an accident. We existed before being born to our parents and we will exist when we shed this body that currently carries us through this world. The earth is a wonderful garden, a self-regulating system saturated with intelligence that we are to share with all creatures.

Yogananda summed it up this way:

A panorama of unity unfolds in an understanding of esoteric truth. Divine incarnations do not come to bring a new or exclusive religion, but to restore the One Religion of God-realization. The great ones, like waves, all bathe in the Eternal Sea and become One with it. The outwardly varying messages of the prophets are part of the necessary relativity that accommodates human diversity. It is narrow-mindedness that creates religious bigotry and divisive denominationalism, constricting truth to ritualistic worship and sectarian dogma; the form is mistaken for the spirit. The essential message of actual contact between man and Maker is diluted with ignorance.

The undreamed-of technical advances in civilization made possible by the splitting of the atom and the harnessing of subatomic energies will ultimately bring all peoples into such close proximity in travel and communication that humanity will have to reevaluate its attitudes. Either persistence in ignorant intolerance will spawn mass suffering, or an openness to the common spiritual link of souls will presage a global well-being of peace and amity. This is a clarion call that the time has come to separate truth from spurious convictions, knowledge from ignorance. The teachings of Jesus as understood in harmony with the revelations of the Great Ones of India will revive the practical methods of the intuitive knowing of truth through Self-realization. Realized truth and scientific knowledge are the sure means to combat the shadowy doubts and superstitions hedging humanity. Only a flood of the light of truth through actual communion with God can dispel the gathered darkness of the ages.

The person who worships reason only and is not conscious of the availability of his power of intuition—by which alone he can know himself as soul—remains little more than a rational animal, out of touch with the spiritual heritage that is his birthright.

The Heavenly Father is the progenitor of every race; His children are duty-bound to love the whole family of nations. Any country that goes against the principle of love for humankind will not long prosper, for lack of international harmony and mutual cooperation puts a nation in conflict not only with its neighbors but with Divine Law, the Organizing Principle of the cosmos. To those in tune with this cosmic heartbeat of coalescent love, God is trying to bring unity in the universe. Those who are in tune with this cosmic beneficence, as was Jesus, have love and understanding that embraces the totality of humanity, setting the standard for all God's children to follow.

To Jesus no one was a stranger; he loved unconditionally, and gauged individuals solely by their inner qualifications; their spiritual sincerity and receptivity to Truth.

The ancient Eastern teachings center on the immortality of the soul as does the Christian doctrine, but they also teach the doctrine of reincarnation; rebirth many times on Earth as a result of desires and working out *Karma*. *Karma* is the mechanism for us to learn the lessons we need to develop to our highest potential. Desire for things and sensual experiences during this incarnation bind us to come back and fulfill that body of desires. Free will and personal responsibility are cornerstones of the Eastern doctrines. We are personally responsible for our thoughts and actions, made with our freedom of choice. Through this long line of rebirth the soul learns and develops fully into the highest form of human being. Jesus was such a perfected human being and he showed us with his life, his teachings, and his actions. The Western world had never seen such a saint.

However many of our behavioral choices are made within the cultural framework we are raised and live within. Doing what we are taught is normal and right. Most human beings want to do what is right. Our hearts tell us the right way to go if we listen to that small still voice, a voice that may be drowned out by the loud voice of our ego and the voices of those around us. If one ignores the inner voice and transgresses the healthy path of behavior, there are side effects for one's *Karma* and one's health.

A further step, on this path, is time spent in private prayer or meditation. The Hindus, Buddhists, and my Unity Church teach meditation techniques. Jesus taught to go into a "closet" and pray inwardly. Learning how to still our minds from focusing upon the outer senses and the outer world we find the inner light of peace, joy, and feel the presence of God.

Jesus in the *Essene Gospel of Peace* directly taught the path of cleansing our minds and bodies. In the New Testament he taught different methods of prayer, right thinking, and action in relation to our fellow man. Jesus came back to his people, the Hebrews, and tried to teach them how to live with *ahimsa.* That is, the Eastern doctrine of causing no harm to the other creatures of Earth and loving your fellow man even those who would do you wrong. Jesus taught the doctrine of giving and sharing with those in need. He taught the path of compassion. This is the path of natural human development towards a higher potential and a higher interaction with the greater powers of the universe.

My grandfather, a Christian scientist, taught me as a

young person that "God is all in all." *Sri Yukteswar* taught in his Chapter 1: The Gospel, Sutra 1:

> The Eternal Father, God, *Swami Parabrahma*, is the only Real Substance, *Sat*, and is all in all in the universe. **Why God is not comprehensible.** Man possesses eternal faith and believes intuitively in the existence of a Substance, of which the objects of sense—sound, touch, sight, taste, and smell, the component parts of this visible world—are but properties. As man identifies himself with his material body, composed of the aforesaid properties, he is able to comprehend by these imperfect organs these properties only, and not the Substance to which these properties belong. The Eternal Father, God, the only Substance in the universe, is therefore not comprehensible by man of this material world, unless he becomes divine by lifting his self above this creation of Darkness or *Maya*. See Hebrews 11:1 and John 8:28.

Eastern teachers call those who choose to follow the spiritual path where their intuitive hearts and minds lead, adepts. Jesus called such people, disciples. One does not have to become a wondering monk to become an adept. You can have a family and a job but some human circumstances are more conducive to produce adepts than others. This is the natural healthy path toward humanity's highest potential. All of us no matter what race, sex, or religion can work toward this higher potential if we choose through our freewill to do so. The world would be a much better place if we would but choose to do so. *Sri Yukteswar* stated it thus:

> Adeptship is attainable by the purification of the body in all respects. Purification of the material body can be effected by things generated along with it by Nature; that of the electric body by the patience in all circum-

stances; and that of the magnetic body (*chitta*, spiritual-ized Atom, Heart) by the regulation of the breath, which is called *mantra*, the purifier of the mind. The process of how these purifications can be effected may be learnt at the feet of the divine personages who witness Light and bear testimony of the Christ Consciousness.

It has been clearly demonstrated in the foregoing pages that "Love is God," not merely as the noblest sen-timent of a poet but as an aphorism of eternal truth. To whatever religious creed a man may belong and what-ever may be his position in society, if he properly culti-vates this ruling principle naturally implanted in his heart, he is sure to be on the right path to save himself from wandering in this creation of Darkness, *Maya*.

I have tried to show through out this book where our an-cient cultural ways come from and how some of them affect us negatively and how their effects upon the larger world around us harm all. As the Hopi grandfathers tell us, we are at a cross-roads and we need to make some big changes in ways we live to alter the course of destruction that we face. We can and we need to live more cooperatively with each other and the larger living systems of the world and beyond. There is great un-tapped human potential waiting to be developed to make this world a better place. We need to get off the path of war and start walking the humble path of peace toward our higher po-tential. We must abandon many old ways and put our minds and hearts together as brothers and sisters, children of the One Universe who can forge a better way.

The wise sage, poet, James Dillet Freeman wrote these words in his story *The Heart Will Find Its Own*:

Without love this existence is life imprisonment. Until loves sets us free, each of us is confined in the narrow prison of himself. Who has never felt that he is bound as by walls? Love bursts these walls of self and selfishness.

For above all love is sharing. Love is a power. Love is a change that takes place in our own heart. Sometimes it may change others, but always it changes us.

Love is to find happiness in making others happy. It is to understand what others think and feel and need. It is to say and do things that make them eager to be with us and to do these things not for the effect but because it is natural for us to do them.

It is to appreciate the importance of others and help them appreciate their own importance.

When some feel that they have love, they have only a word. It is easy to say that we love strangers when they are far from us or that we love God when God is but a shadowy abstraction. But when the stranger knocks at our heart and cries "Share!"—when God becomes the disturber of our soul who answers, "Serve!"—then we find out if we truly love.

For those who have never given, it is not easy to give. Let them begin by giving but a little. Let them give a smile where they would have passed unheeding. Let them give a kind word where they would not have spoken.

If you will take one faltering step, love will rush to meet you and bear you on. For love is the great giver.

There is a power that links the Earth and Sun and binds the stars together into galaxies, a power that binds the segments of life into a perfect whole. Alone in our little self, we feel our incompleteness. We know in our heart that we are part of something more.

Love is the power that links the lonely islands of men's souls, beaten by icy separating seas of ignorance and fear and circumstance. Love is the power that links us all in God, as all the islands are linked in the Earth. Yet love is not a chain. Love is completion.

So go now, develop yourself on this healthy path, find your peace, and discover your greater joy in a better future. Peace be with you.

Bibliography

Ambrose, Stephen E. *Undaunted Courage* New York: Touchstone, 1996.

Anderson, Fred. *George Washington Remembers* Lanham: Rowan & Littlefield, 2004.

Barker, A.T. *The Mahatma Letters* Pasadena: Theosophical University Press, 1975.

Bodge, George Madison. *Soldiers in King Philip's War* originally published Boston 1906. Reprinted by the Baltimore Genealogical Publishing, 2002.

Coard, Michael. *The "Black" Eye of George Washington's "White' House"* Philadelphia: Avenging the Ancestors Coalition, 2005.

Darwin, Charles. *The Origin of Species* Chicago: Encyclopedia Britannica, Inc., 1952

Deardorff, James W. *A New Ecumenism Based Upon Reexamination of the "Lost Years" Evidence* Oregon State University, 1994 found at www.proaxis.com/~deardorj/ecumensm.htm

Ereira, Alan. *The Elder Brothers* New York: Alfred A. Knopf, 1992.

Fischer, David Hackett. *Albion's Seed* New York: Oxford University Press, 1989.

Freeman, James Dillet. *Angels Sing In Me* Unity Village, Missouri: Unity House, 2004.

Fromm, Eric. *To Have or to Be?* New York: Bantam, 1976.

Great, Aelfred the. *Anglo-Saxon Chronicle.* Translation by Rev. James Ingram. London, 1823.

Green, John Richard. *A Short History of the English People.* New York: American Book Company, 1916.

Grierson, Sir Herbert. *The English Bible.* London: William Collins, 1930.

Grossman, Dave. *On Killing.* Boston, New York, Toronto, London: Back Bay Books, 1995.

Issacs, Harold. *No Peace for Asia.* New York; 1947 in *Vietnam.* Gettleman, Marvin. Greenwich: Fawcett Crest, 1965.

James, King. *Holy Bible.* London: Oxford, date unknown

Johnson, Chalmers. *The Sorrows of Empire.* New York: Metropolitian, 2004.

Kiel, R. Andrew. *J. Edgar Hoover—The Father of the Cold War.* Lanham, Maryland: University Press of America, 2000.

Lepore, Jill. *The Name of War. King Philip's War and the Origins of the American Identity.* New York: Alfred A. Knopf, 1999.

Lucy, Sam. *The Anglo-Saxon Way of Death.* Pheonix Mill, UK: Sutton Publishing Limited, 2000.

Macchio, Joseph P. *The Orthodox Suppression of Original Christianity.* Found at http://essenes.net/CouncilOfNicea .html

Manitonquat (Medicine Story). *Return to Creation.* Spokane: Bear Tribe Publishing 1991.

Mann, Barbara Alice. *George Washington's War on Native America.* Westport: Praeger, 2005.

Marshall, George N. *Challenge of a Liberal Faith.* Boston, MA: Pyramid Publications for the Church of the Larger Fellowship, Unitarian Universalist 1975.

McTaggart, Lynne. *The Field: The Quest for the Secret Force of the Universe.* New York, New York: HarperCollins, 2002.

Minh, Ho Chi. *La Vie Ouvriere. Selected Works.* Hanoi: 1962 p.62–65 in Vietnam. Gettleman, Marvin. Greenwich; Fawcett Crest, 1965.

Nennius, the lowly minister and servant of the servants of God, by the grace of God, disciple of St. Elbotus, to all the followers of truth sendeth health. *Historia Brittonum.* 8th Century. Source: *Six Old English Chronicles.* London, 1848.

Pelteret, David. *Slave Raiding and Slave Trading in Early England.* Journal of Anglo Saxon England

Sahtouris, Elisabet. *Earthdance: Living Systems in Evolution.* Lincoln, NE: iUniversity Press, 2000.

Stenton, Sir Frank. *Anglo-Saxon England.* London: Oxford University Press, 1975.

Szekely, Edmond Bordeaux. *The Essene Gospel of Peace.* International Biogenic Society, 1981.

Tacitus. *The Agricola and Germania.* A.J. Church and W.J. Brodribb, translators. London: Macmillan, 1877.

Ward, Christopher. *The War of the Revolution.* New York: The Macmillan Company, 1952.

Waters, Frank. *The Book of Hopi.* New York: Viking Press 1978.

Yogananda, Paramahansa. *Autobiography of a Yogi.* Los Angeles: Self Realization Fellowship, 1972.

Yogananda, Paramahansa. *The Second Coming of Christ.* Los Angeles: Self Realization Fellowship, 2004.

Yukteswar, Swami Sri. *The Holy Science.* Los Angles: Self Realization Fellowship, 1990.

Zinn, Howard. *A People's History of the United States.* New York: Harper Perennial, 1980.

ABOUT THE AUTHOR

George Hiram Williston is currently a high school shop teacher in a small farming community in Michigan. He is also a professional cabinetmaker/woodworker. His interest in the history of Christianity, the nature of Jesus, esoteric Buddhism, Hinduism, Native American writers and American History are at the core of *This Tribe of Mine*. George recently characterized his philosophy: " I feel a need to help in healing humanity and the Earth. We must stop endless war. My belief is that all people are basically good. So we must change the culture and what it is teaching to change individual behaviors."

His first book is a step in the right direction for change.